Moving far beyond the confine
humankind is now poised at a
development that will usher in
psychic abilities.

By the same author:

OUT-OF-BODY EXPERIENCES: A Handbook

CONSCIOUS EVOLUTION

Understanding Extrasensory Abilities in Everyday Life

Janet Lee Mitchell, Ph.D.

Aquarian/Thorsons
An Imprint of HarperCollins*Publishers*

The Aquarian Press
An Imprint of HarperCollins*Publishers*
77-85 Fulham Palace Road,
Hammersmith, London W6 8JB

Published by The Aquarian Press 1992
First published in the USA by Ballantine Books,
a division of Random House, Inc., 1989
1 3 5 7 9 10 8 6 4 2

© Janet Lee Mitchell, Ph.D., 1989

Janet Lee Mitchell asserts the moral right to
be identified as the author of this work

A catalogue record for this book
is available from the British Library

ISBN 1 85538 083 8

Printed in Great Britain by
HarperCollinsManufacturing Glasgow

All rights reserved. No part of this publication may be
reproduced, stored in a retrieval system, or transmitted,
in any form or by any means, electronic, mechanical,
photocopying, recording or otherwise, without the prior
permission of the publishers.

To
Rev. Doris Kean Carter

She aided my conscious evolution
through unconditional love,
understanding, and gentle compassion.

"It is only with the heart that one can see rightly;
what is essential is invisible to the eye."

—ANTOINE DE SAINT-EXUPÉRY
The Little Prince

TABLE OF CONTENTS

ACKNOWLEDGMENTS

The Reverend Doris Kean Carter was a dear friend for 18 years. She sponsored my conscious evolution in every sense of the word. When I was arrogant, she showed me things I didn't know. When I was ignorant, she taught me how life works with perfect justice even when daily encounters might not seem fair. Her image of me was truly what I wanted to be, and she held onto my dreams when I was too weak to stand.

I wrote this book shortly after I relocated to Cottonwood, Arizona, after living in New York City for twenty-three years. The first thing I missed was access to good books. Richard Chase had a bookstore in town, and when he went out of business, he asked if he could store about 1,500 volumes in my house. A week after this wonderful library was placed in my house, I was asked to write this book. I couldn't have done it without the library, or without Richard's support. Interestingly enough, about a week after I finished the manuscript (unbeknownst to Richard) he called and said he would like to come and get his books back. Right on time, Richard!

I would like to add my special thanks to Adair Edwards for her reading of the manuscript, and for her kind encouragement. Others who read parts of the book and commented on it were Marian Nester, Al Sabin, Shirley Smith, Marcie Stevenson, and Winifred Stryker. And, of course, none of this could have been accomplished without the enthusiastic support of an extremely evolved editor, Cheryl Woodruff.

INTRODUCTION

I usually like to know something of a person's background and biases before I consider their opinions. This book may challenge you to think about things you haven't thought much about before or to think about them in a different way. I want you to be challenged and to react or respond to the things you will be reading as if you were in a debate with me. Don't take anything I say for granted. Experiment with the ideas yourself, and if they work, use them.

This is not a strictly scientific book. It is an impassioned personal view of the blocks and resistances some people seem to encounter when faced with exploring their innate potential. The release and development of this potential is exactly what I think is at stake when all our human abilities are not allowed full expression. We are at a crossroads in human evolution, and our old ways of solving problems no longer work. Yet, the stakes have never been higher, for the traditional structures of our society are collapsing around us.

First, and foremost, I consider myself to be a creative, invisible being who owns a body. I contend that we are living under a false notion of what being human is all about. I agree with Teilhard de Chardin's theory that nature forever seeks higher complexity and higher consciousness, and that we humans are the highest form of this conscious evolution on the planet.

The purpose of this book is to help shift the creative process in which we are all participating onto a more conscious level. Only when we become conscious of our intuitive and creative abilities will we be able to join together to create a reality that is more to our liking.

The Education of a "Religious Scientist"

When I was a child, I attended various protestant religious services almost daily. I was not forced to attend church, but I'd been told that I might like it. And, in fact, there was something there that definitely appealed to me. The ideas that we have souls and live after this life were fascinating to my innate curiosity. When I saw how people who became converted were transformed, I listened carefully to their testimonies to hear how the presence of God affected their daily lives. I was already a "religious scientist" but, of course, I didn't know there was such a thing at the time.

I was born in West Virginia, and lived there until I was nineteen years of age. I never heard people mention extrasensory perception (ESP) as such, but my mother told me that people thought if you dreamed a dream on a certain night and then told it to someone, it would come true. She told me she'd had such a dream, told it, and that it had indeed come true that very week. The dream foretold the death of someone she knew.

I heard about babies being "born with a veil" and they were spoken of as having a "sixth sense." There was an innate understanding that one could influence material reality, but no one knew exactly how this was done. I also heard of places being haunted. And, once, an image was reported to have materialized on a house and many people went to see it. Unfortunately, I did not get to go despite my rabid curiosity and persistence—two qualities that have always been basic to my concept of myself.

It was in church that I first got a glimpse of invisible reality. Somehow I felt those were the ideas I was going to be interested in for the rest of my life, even though for a while I couldn't make my religion work for me because my understanding of the fundamentalist terminology got in the way of any practical application of the principles.

The older I got, the more the message from the churches seemed to be telling me that I was inadequate. As I entered my teens, my life became increasingly stressful. But, stuck in the role of "worthless sinner," I couldn't seem to get any help from a tyrannical God isolated somewhere in the sky. I began to feel that God didn't care about me anymore. The truth was, I couldn't care about anything anymore—it was too painful and confusing. For eight years I felt separated from God.

In 1962, I met Dr. Raymond Charles Barker and became an avid student of Religious Science for the next eleven years. Within twenty minutes of the first talk I attended, I knew this was the information I had been seeking. In one class I was told to stand, arms out to the side, eyes closed, and try to sense where my nose was or the tips of my fingers. Then I was instructed to find out who was making these observations. It was a dramatic meeting with myself as "perfect spiritual being" after only being identified with my personality and behavior up to this point. The teachings helped me see myself as a creative, invisible being, connected with all life and important to it. This knowledge helped me clarify my thinking about God and my relationship with the universe.

As I began to practice the spiritual principles outlined in these classes, grace began to flow freely in my life. (The whole concept of grace is extremely important. If you don't know what grace is, there is an excellent discussion at the end of M. Scott Peck's book, *The Road Less Traveled*, that relates grace to the ideas presented in this book on ESP and conscious evolution.) As I stopped resisting the workings of grace, events in my life took on a mystical quality. People were wonderful and helpful to me, and everything about my life seemed to improve.

Every day for the next five years, I asked to be shown who I was and what I was to do. I was especially interested in the directions my work life would take because I loved to work. I could say today that I was looking for a professional objective, but at that time I had no idea I could have a profession. It still sounded like something only men had. Even though I put on a good act in my office job, I knew I was not a secretary. But I didn't know about other positions that might be open to women as I had come from a very limited background where women were wives, waitresses, or telephone operators.

Finding My Path

One night on television I saw a program about parapsychologists in a laboratory, and I knew, without a doubt, that was the field I had been searching for. It is important to note that the answer to my spiritual question came through watching TV. Your answers may come from a place you would least expect. Don't rule out any possible source.

Parapsychology was beckoning, but I'd had very little formal education. I had taken a stenographic course in high school, which led to my job as a secretary, and that had taught me how to write letters. So I wrote to ESP experimenters in the area and volunteered my services. I took a course in parapsychology at The New School for Social Research and another at New York University in order to meet psychic researchers and gain knowledge. One year later I was employed at the American Society for Psychical Research as a manuscript typist and general flunky. I began to absorb information like a sponge. However, my supervisor informed me that without an education, my dreams of being a psychic researcher were in vain. And so, at age 31, before and after work, I began attending high school classes for college prerequisite courses, as well as taking college courses.

Four years later I graduated with a B.A. in Psychology from Hunter College. Six months later I found myself enrolled in a Ph.D. program at the City College of New York, studying under one of the most qualified researchers in parapsychology. I hardly knew what a Ph.D. was, but I knew I wanted to do research and do it right. Perseverance and dedication helped me overcome many obstacles to remain on course in pursuit of my academic and career goals. Veterans' benefits, part-time jobs, scholarships, fellowships, grants, and loans were always there when I needed them. It felt as if this was the will of God for my life. At age 45, I received a Doctorate in Experimental Cognition from the City University of New York.

By this time I had been doing laboratory research on ESP for fifteen years. I had studied ESP and meditation, telepathy, clairvoyance, biofeedback and other physiological measuring techniques, psychokinesis (PK), and the relationship between various cognitive styles and ESP abilities. My purpose was becoming clear. I wanted to help advance human understanding of the essential self and its scope of abilities.

I did pioneering research on perceptual and psychophysiological aspects of out-of-body experiences, establishing standards for work in an area that many considered beyond methodology. I helped build a solid foundation for serious, controlled, and systematic research for the study of these types of ephemeral human experiences.

As I continued to develop conscious clarity about who I was and what I was to do, life became a great adventure. I realized that it had been my privilege over the years to be able to do exactly what I wanted to do. As a result, I decided to write about and share my investigations on out-of-body experiences. I compiled ten years of library and laboratory research into as concise a form as I could so people would have access to what we know today about a human ability that few are willing to consider seriously. The book was entitled OUT-OF-BODY EXPERIENCES: A HANDBOOK (New York: Ballantine Books, 1981), and it was very well received. It is reaching more readers today than it did when it was first published.

We Are Life Itself

In CONSCIOUS EVOLUTION I will share with you some of the insights that have come to me over the years. I will offer you facts that have been meaningful in my own conscious evolutionary process. I will try to help you learn what to look for and how to look for it. In sharing my experience, I hope and trust that your experience of life and all it has to offer will be enhanced.

I make no discrimination between spiritual growth and conscious evolution. In nature, there is an indefinable something that is always seeking greater expression, which we can see by the acceleration of change that we have experienced in just the last 50 years in this country. I believe that human beings are instruments—to the extent they will allow—for that greater expression; that the phrase, "in nature," could be another of the names of God. In fact, "GOD" could be an acronym for *g*ood *o*rderly *d*irection. I no longer have an anthropomorphic concept of God, but the word is still acceptable to me. My concept of God has changed several times as I have become more consciously evolved, and I am willing for it to change again if it will bring more life to my body and experience.

I believe we are made in the image and likeness of God, with dignity, but that until we get back to this self-image, we are going to stumble around in the darkness of ignorance, unaware of our true capabilities. Abraham Maslow was one of the first psychologists to study spiritual experiences and he concluded: "It is precisely the God-like in ourselves that we are ambivalent about, fascinated by, and fearful of; motivated to and defensive against."

The importance of this self-image cannot be underestimated. As long as we see ourselves as this needy material form that is separated from everything it needs, we will continue to try to function under the rules of "survival of the fittest" and "the one with the most is the best."

Once we understand that we are not separated from everything that is, we may come to realize that, in fact, we are everything. There is nothing we have to get *from* life—we *are* life itself. From this point of enlightened self-awareness, working together we can make this reality we share whatever we want it to be. It becomes possible to find solutions to problems once we truly understand that they can be transcended.

If just one person at a time adopts the self-image of a creative, invisible being, and gains increasing awareness and power over stubborn viewpoints and limited circumstances—and then that person teaches at least one other person (there are, after all, only five billion of us on the planet)—how long could it take given our present rapid communication systems? We have to understand that we translate our mental concepts into physical form and, based on that information, choose carefully what conceptions we wish to materialize.

The Fear Barrier

Science and religion meld together for me. Today I consider myself a scientist who studies religious concepts in the laboratory. I think parapsychology could be the perfect blend between science and religion. However, since any emerging science is in great fear of being discredited, few parapsychologists are willing to jeopardize their positions by using such words as "God" and "oneness." There are approximately 300 parapsychologists in the world, and I do not feel they are fulfilling their responsibility to lead us forward into the practical application of our expanded human abilities. At this crucial point in our development we need bold conscious evolutionary researchers.

When I was doing research at a university, they were quite interested in my ideas on psychokinesis and asked me how I thought it worked. Of course, we do not know a great deal about the process of PK at this point; we only know that humans can somehow affect matter at a distance. So, I told them I thought there was probably a basic unity to life, and that one could transcend the idea of separation. My most credible scientific colleague blurted out, "Don't tell me you believe in God, too?" I replied that I had an idea there was something somewhere that knew more than I did.

It is not unusual in my work to encounter this kind of resistance. This is an example of the pervasiveness of the antispirituality stance of academia. Our fear of the power of our own minds and our adherence to traditional ways of thinking and acting get in the way of our venturing forward in our conscious evolutionary process.

A parapsychological breakthrough that will lead to human beings accepting and learning to use their expanded human abilities is probably not going to happen through academic or other traditional channels of research because people are afraid. We are victims of psychophobia. Some people are afraid because their religious background tells them that any kind of extended abilities are linked with the occult and black magic. Some people are afraid because they think it contradicts their traditional religious beliefs—without even beginning to explore the reality that many of the gifts and miracles performed by Jesus—when we look at them from the parapsychological perspective—reflect expanded human capacities.

We are not only separated from others in our thoughts, we are even cut off from our own lives. For instance, one may think, "If I live creatively, expressing myself as I choose, I probably won't be able to make a living" or, "If I have a good home life, I can't have a successful career." This kind of thinking forces us to make choices that reduce us to living only a fragment of our full selves. We limit ourselves by thinking we can only be effective in one dimension of reality instead of realizing we can be even more successful as fully developed multidimensional beings. We exhaust and frustrate ourselves by rebelling against these narrow constructs of dehumanized life, for the dominant model we live under dehumanizes us. Without conscious evolution there is no hope for regaining our human spirit and greatness.

The Promise of Self-Consciousness

The ideas of physical evolution that say we are a higher animal form and have such and such brain capacity—based on studies of rats' brains—form the basis of our limited ideas of how we solve problems and survive. These ideas are no longer working. It is now becoming clearer and clearer that we have to find a new way to live life to the fullest. We are conscious beings, not merely evolved animals. While our brains may be similar to a rat's brain in structure, our consciousness is not. The rat is conscious; we are self-conscious. That means the rat acts from need and is not conscious of the purpose of its actions. Although humans act out of need too, they are also conscious of those needs and actions. We can form concepts about possible actions, and we can also change the concept without having to take the action. We can influence our surroundings, be aware of that influence, and change it at will. We can think abstractly, concretely, or functionally. We can place our attention on whatever we choose in thought or form, and carry out our intention to perform in certain ways. One cannot generalize from a rat's brain to a human's brain and intelligently discuss the thoughts, actions, and influence of self-conscious beings.

In order to solve our current problems we have to open ourselves to information from invisible realms. Now, all of us have to allow ourselves to be inspired to envision our future reality using all the gifts of the most creative and inventive minds of the past.

We have role models throughout history for these visionary methods. Our literature is filled with examples. You will see acknowledgments to muses or to a greater source, or mentions of being divinely inspired, or of letting an idea incubate in a dream.

This kind of creative power, this ability to creatively synthesize new answers, is the gift that awaits our becoming involved in the process of conscious evolution. This is why I want people to read this book. I want everyone to partake of the rich universe of possibilities available to us all. The evolutionary frontier for the 21st century is the acknowledgment and exploration of the treasures of our inner space and learning to translate what we find into how we live our daily lives. The recognition of our innate expanded human abilities is the current challenge of human consciousness.

The last great event to take place in this society occurred in 1969 when Neil Armstrong stepped on the moon. A whole generation has missed the thrill of this kind of accomplishment. It is my feeling that great ideas are being suppressed or not expressed because of our total immersion in superficial competition on commercial, materially focused levels. A paradigm shift is needed to free us from this competitive hysteria, and to enable us to discover our innate potential. In the new paradigm there is no reason for competition—only cooperation.

Owning Our God Selves

We live in a highly verbal society where there is considerable talk about how wonderful things are. This makes us complacent and much less likely to take the steps necessary to make our lives all they can be. We have elevated the illusion of objective reality to an almost God-like position. To be objective or verbal is to be considered "better" in this society. People with performance skills, as opposed to verbal skills, have always been downgraded and paid less, and they are getting sick and tired of it. This is why we often can't get anything accomplished—it is equally, if not more important, to do something as to say something.

In reality there is no such thing as pure objectivity, let's stop kidding ourselves. Scientists, from psychologists to physicists, know that merely observing an event has a profound influence on the event. Our empowerment and the ability to live a fully actualized, healthy and happy life come from going completely into the subjective realms, taking knowledge gained there, and using it in our external relationships. Empowerment comes from that depth.

There is no reason for us to be threatened by the idea—or the reality—of a fully evolved life. Exploring this challenge can propel us into a new understanding of how we evolve as conscious beings, without disregarding how we evolve as physical beings. We do not give up the physical for the conscious—it is an added dimension. When we correct wrong assumptions our worlds expand; they do not shrink or deteriorate.

As we consider the ideas in this book, we are adding knowledge to what we already know. We are physical beings, but what makes us unique on the planet is that we can have an impact on our surroundings and be conscious of it. Science has focused our attention on our physical evolution for over a hundred years. Now, let's focus some attention on what makes a human different from an animal—our consciousness. Our society gets a lot more useful information from the scientists who are attempting to teach chimpanzees to communicate with us than we do from scientists who are examining how our language molds our experience and vice versa. Let's examine whether there truly is "power in the spoken word" and how we might make that work for us to improve our life condition.

The dynamic tension between flow and control is having a profound impact on how we live our lives. The old model taught us that we must control and subjugate matter—and human beings—at any cost. The new model demands that we acknowledge that our survival can only be insured by learning to flow in harmony with all the various life forces around us. Unless we realize the connectedness of all substance, of all life forms, our self-destructive lifestyle will continue. Sheer physical survival was a necessary goal at one point in our evolution. But today it is not enough.

Now we need to know who we are and how we operate. We can no longer be content to grind along as cogs in some vast, impersonal machine.

It is important to our conscious evolutionary process that we acknowledge the existence of something larger than ourselves, something with more knowledge and more power than ourselves. The next step is to realize that there is no separation between us and that source.

Once you are consciously connected—wait, watch and listen. You will receive instruction in some form and, in time, you will recognize true guidance as opposed to ego gratification. Trust your inner guidance and follow it for the most fascinating adventure of your life.

It is my hope that by getting involved with your own conscious evolutionary process, you may experience some of these rewards:

You will no longer feel yourself a prisoner in your body.

You will not be a captive to your thoughts or chained to fleeting emotions.

You will have an experience of ecstasy or bliss (regardless of its duration).

You will let go of the useless ideas of the arguing intellect and yield to intuition as a superior way of knowing.

You will be able to observe your thoughts, emotions, and bodily sensations in order to become more consciously involved in your daily experience.

You will recognize your own personal truth, intuitively understand its significance, and know what to do about it.

Your attitude towards things, people, and events will gradually change and open.

You will begin to express qualities you had only read or heard about before.

You will experience a permanent improvement in the quality of your life.

You will allow something wonderful to be achieved through you, and you will joyously accept the rewards of that achievement.

Anxiety will subside and courage will prevail.

Chapter I

EVOLUTION VERSUS DEATH

Today most of us live with the fear of death or denial of it. Nuclear technology appears to be getting out of control and the earth could be obliterated in short order. There are hundreds of computer errors per year involving nuclear weapons activation. Sometimes an error is detected only moments before a nuclear attack might be initiated. Nuclear power plants and other high-tech facilities pollute the air, ground, water, and everything in between, and average citizens usually feel helpless to stop this desecration of our homes.

We are also confronting the worst epidemic in medical history—one that is gaining on us daily—the AIDS virus. The National Academy of Sciences warned us in 1986: "Starting in 1990, the disease AIDS will kill as many Americans each year as the Vietnam War killed in an entire decade—58,000." Sad to say, this statistic is probably conservative and misleading. In 1989 Dr. Mathilde Krim, founding cochair of the American Foundation for AIDS Research, announced that there were 90,990 reported cases of AIDS in the U.S., with over 2,000,000 people *known* to be infected with the virus. In 1984, ten cases of AIDS were diagnosed per day in America; in 1985, it rose to 35 per day; and in 1986, there were 58 cases per day. Conservative projections suggest that a quarter million cases could be diagnosed in America in the year 1991. In 1989, more women than men are being infected with the virus. Women are also being infected with another virus (HPV: human papilloma virus) in epidemic proportions. This is another sexually transmitted disease, and it has been estimated that 38,000 people per day are contracting some form of sexually transmitted disease, from herpes to AIDS.

We live in a society that is falling apart. Nothing works anymore. Our cars don't work; our schools don't work; our intimate relationships don't work; our houses don't work; our governments don't work; our lives don't work. We've reached a crisis point where we can no longer depend on someone out there to do it for us and make it all better.

A Question of Survival

When any organism is faced with awesome environmental demands, the choices for its survival are pretty straightforward. So, too, are the choices that face us in the days ahead: either we grow and adapt, or we will die. We are now faced with environmental, social, and economic demands beyond anything human beings have ever experienced in the past.

There are an estimated 18,000,000 alcoholics in this country alone. In 1988, National Institute on Drug Abuse officials reported 5,000 new cocaine users daily and an estimated 7,000,000 regular and compulsive users ("Drugs: Running the Numbers," *Science*, 6/24/89, p. 1729). This is approximately one-tenth of our population. People want to anesthetize themselves because they can't bear to watch what is happening to their lives. These individuals are not only destroying themselves but the family structure of our society. The havoc that this is creating in the lives of young people is pushing Americans to the brink of their own self-destruction from within.

The high school dropout rate in 1986 was 4,318,000, and over 90 percent of high school seniors have used some form of alcohol or drugs. In 1983, 109 out of 1,000 females between the ages of 15 and 19 became pregnant. About half of these (51.7) gave birth *(U.S. News & World Report*, 11/16/87, p. 84). The pregnancy rate is rising in the age group from 10 to 15. Teenagers are bringing babies into the world without any supporting family structure at an alarming rate and no one seems to know how to stop it. Our young people are growing up in a culture that seems hell-bent on destroying the material world and our bodies with it. Where is the reverence for life most of us seem to agree is so vital to human survival?

Most of this destruction stems from greed and distorted ideas of power. By "power" we mean the ability of one group to enslave and control another. "Greed" is the belief that power belongs to whoever has the most material goods, especially money. These are false ideas that lead to domination and to a hunger for wealth that is never satisfied.

And yet, in the midst of this seeming apathy and indifference, a revolution of human thought is occurring as more and more people are becoming concerned about their own individual health, a healthy environment, and by extension, world health. We are beginning to recognize ourselves as indispensable elements of nature. *We* are becoming the environment to worry about most. We need to discover in ourselves the source of wonder and delight that we might experience while gazing at a beautiful sunset or listening to waves crashing on the shore in such precision and order. As we identify with the power of nature, we might find it within ourselves to create movements for the protection of ourselves as the most valuable, endangered species on this planet.

The death of the material should not concern us so much since our physical existence is temporary at best. However, the death of the spirit is quite another matter. One bumper sticker put it succinctly: "The problem in America today is apathy; but who cares." There is not so much talk and concern about this spiritual death we are experiencing right now because it is so alarming we have, to a large extent, blocked our view of it. Instead of becoming aware of what is happening now, we look with fear to the future and our possible physical extinction. In some ways this is a distraction—a diversion for our own comfort. We will all experience physical death sooner or later; it is inevitable. Yet, when we focus our attention on the fear of some moment in the future, we rob ourselves of whatever beauty, love, and joy we might experience in the present.

It is natural to sometimes feel hopeless and useless in the face of imminent death. However, if numbness of fear has removed us from the moment, we cannot build the future we desire. It is what we do today that governs what tomorrow will be. If we have gone unconscious under the pressure of fear, we will be content to let life happen to us. If we recognize our true essence and its desire for a quality life on all levels, then those qualities can happen through us.

The state of denial brought on by fear has to be transcended if we are to become the conscious beings we were meant to be. We are not only conscious of our experiences, but can actually direct them. This is what makes human beings unique on this planet. And yet, to a large extent, we are not currently employing our unique abilities in a conscious fashion. For most of us our expanded human abilities (ESP, creativity, hunches) come into play in a random way and we do not acknowledge or own them. We feel they just sort of happen to us. However, the magnitude of the world's problems at this time demands that we harness our full potential to the best of our ability and bring it to bear on these crisis situations.

What Is Evolution: A Darwinian View

Evolution strives for quality, efficiency, beauty, and cooperation. It is an idea that has been of interest to all civilizations and all historical periods, including Chinese, Babylonian, Egyptian, and Greek, and from ancient times to the medieval period, and from the Renaissance up to the present. In the 19th century, the concept of evolution became a topic of serious scientific discussion. Darwin's theory of natural selection was based on the idea that there must be a struggle for existence. The impact of Darwin's deduction on social and economic thinking has been unfortunate in some ways. His idea of "survival of the fittest" has been misinterpreted by many to mean survival by winning wars and competitions. This, in turn, has led to selfish rationalizations and the attitude that it's everyone for him or herself in social and economic affairs.

Darwinian theory, as applied to biology in particular, may be seen as an exhausted, 120-year search in the wrong direction. *It will probably be revealed to be a largely inadequate explanation of human evolution. The time to look elsewhere for evolutionary data is long overdue.*

Litvak and Senzee wrote "The Evolving Brain" in 1986 and examined evolutionary theory:

> The importance of providing an alternative world view to that of Darwinism has not been stressed enough, probably because it is not widely recognized how deeply an implied Darwinian philosophy

has permeated our culture, values, thinking, and behavior....

Evolution is the transcending reality of life. In the mystic's parlance it is the "unfolding of the moment." It is change in its most profound sense—at once process and progress. We are in a season of human history that is most favorable and crucial for the planting of new evolutionary seeds of thought. With proper care and attention, the resulting yield can provide ample abundance and an improved outlook for all of us, as well as for those to come.... The aim [of evolution] is movement into even greater reality.[1]

The process of evolution is not all "dog eat dog." It is true that evolution favors those who are complex individually. It favors humans because we are capable of further complexity by cooperation among ourselves and because we are mobile in an environment that continually poses threats and challenges. However, quite clearly, plants have evolved without bloody wars. While competition is part of the process, cooperation is also an essential element to survival. Natural selection not only evolves from survival of the fittest, but from survival of those forms that are best integrated with the various elements of the environment in which they live.

Jule Eisenbud, who is Associated Clinical Professor of Psychiatry at the University of Colorado Medical School and a practicing psychoanalyst, writes that Darwin's theories of natural selection do not explain certain complexities of evolution that work on an all-or-nothing basis. He also hypothesizes that ecological factors may cause some members of a species to "agree," through some sort of psychic influence, to be the ones killed by predators or accidents for purposes of population control.

Many different tribes have worked on this last assumption by employing magical ceremonies before setting out on a hunt in order to get the animals to come to them, and "agree" to be used for the tribe's food needs. Long-distance hypnosis has also worked under certain controlled conditions.

Today, most evolutionary theories come from biological considerations where *the process of evolution is seen to involve a change in the characteristics of a species* (usually not human) and the formation of new species. The amount of evidence for organic evolution is tremendous, although much remains to be learned about its mechanisms. Yet, to truly study human evolution, one cannot exclude consciousness or human experiences. One wonders why biological evolution is taught in schools, but not conscious evolution. Self-consciousness is the special trait that separates humans from other life forms. Shouldn't we learn to appreciate this and explore it? Naming and categorizing experiences is not enough; they need to be investigated in depth with a goal of understanding of our innate human potential.

Cultural Evolution

There is also cultural evolution. The human ability to transmit knowledge by language allows us to exercise control over our environment. We can determine the future course of our evolution by instituting purpose and intention. If our purpose is self-destruction, we can also do that—and that is the track we have been on for some time now. Christian dogma ends with a doomsday threat. As a result, many people ask: If Armageddon is all we have to look forward to, why bother? Why? Because responsibility for what happens in the future belongs to each one of us now.

Freud: Psychological Evolution

People in Western society are generally interested in psychology, and most specifically in Freudian theory.

Let's take a brief look at how psychology has evolved and made its impact on our culture. When Darwin triumphed in the mid–19th century, religion gradually began to lose favor among intellectuals. Psychology came to be regarded not as a study of the psyche, but as a science of "mind," another word for "soul" in their terminology.

The first psychological laboratory was established in Germany in 1897 by Wilhelm Wundt. He argued against the reality of a soul and was convinced that our awareness of a "self" was nothing more than the sum total of our various bodily feelings and images. He basically performed psychophysical experiments, measuring reaction times to various stimuli, checking attention span, and studying memory problems.

In 1892, American psychologist William James[2] began to speak of "states of consciousness" and was an advocate of "introspective observation." Introspection means "to look inside," to examine one's own mind or its contents; to engage in an examination of one's thought processes and sensory experiences. James asserted that introspective observation is what human beings have to rely on first, foremost, and always. Such ideas were well received initially, but they soon fell out of fashion when they came up against J.B. Watson's theory of behaviorism.

Watson's book, *Behaviorism*, published in 1924, attempted to shift the image of human beings as conscious, thinking beings possessed of freedom of choice, to one of human beings as caged animals simply responding to stimuli. B.F. Skinner's operant conditioning and stimulus-response theories are modern examples of Watson's influence. Skinner's major thesis is that human perception and behavior are fashioned by particular rewards and punishments or reinforcements that we have received. He views our lives as determined by cultural factors, rather than as an expression of our innate potential. In other words, he sees individual behavior as an effect of the environment rather than a cause of it. Early behaviorists are educated/trained not to concern themselves with any subjective feelings, ideas, sensations, or perceptions. Their vocabulary did not include desire and purpose. Their objective was to observe behavior and to shape it to conform to the prescribed pattern of stimulus and response. The ultimate goal was the control and manipulation of human reactions, as well as other natural phenomena.

Just a point of interest—Watson launched his behaviorist revolution in 1912. In 1920, eight years later, he took a job in advertising. We are still suffering from his psychological sales pitch. One example of this idea's success is the effect of brainwashing techniques.

Watson was influenced by Ivan Pavlov's work in Russia around the turn of the century in which dogs were conditioned to salivate at the sound of a bell. Psychologists do not win Nobel Prizes, but Pavlov, considered a physiological psychologist, did get the prize. His views of human behavior were related to brain function. It is interesting to note that behaviorism has had its greatest impact in Russia and the U.S.A.

In Europe a different approach to the problems of the mind was taking shape. Sigmund Freud and his contemporary Joseph Breuer, a specialist in hypnosis, founded psychoanalysis around 1895. They came into conflict with one another's ideas supposedly because Freud believed that sexual issues lay at the root of most mental disorders. Freud also then theorized that the subconscious mind is some sort of container, or holding zone, where desires or impulses too painful or unpleasant for the conscious mind to acknowledge are repressed. We can "suppress" something consciously; but if we "repress" something, it is unknown to us. Freud also believed that these repressed contents of the unconscious are so powerful that they struggle to express themselves, often emerging in overt neurotic behavior.

While psychoanalysis and behaviorism appear different in theory, they both seem to take for granted that living organisms always act to reduce tension. Freud's "pleasure principle" and behaviorial psychologist Clark Hull's "drive-reduction" theory are very similar. *Both theoretical constructs maintain a strictly biological view of humans, which asserts that humans act only in pursuit of pleasure or to avoid pain.*

These disciplines, by their premises, tend to rob us of our natural wholeness and the power of self-consciousness. *It is important to realize that human beings not only seek survival at this present stage of human evolution, but we seek knowledge of our natural power and how to express it in our daily lives.*

Many people have been convinced that our lives are basically determined by our early conditioning. Watson saw *creative, spiritual, or artistic expressions as trial and error behavior in the search for a satisfying result* (like a rat looking for food); *Freud viewed such behavior as expressions of repressed sexuality.*

Most of the major psychiatrists of the early 20th century denied the reality of the human soul as a distinct immaterial presence.

In 1962 Sir Cyril Burt put it this way: "...psychology, having first bargained away its soul and then gone out of its mind, seems now, as it faces an untimely end, to have lost all consciousness."

People once imagined themselves to be incarnate immortal souls, possessing freedom of choice over their own actions, and destined to survive the dissolution of their physical bodies. Today, after all our scientific enlightenment, we often regard ourselves as mere automatons, victims of heredity and environment, slaves of our animal instincts.

Ironically, when Freud was 65 years old, he wrote in a letter to Hereward Carrington:

> I do not belong with those who reject in advance the study of so-called occult phenomena as being unscientific, unworthy or harmful. If I were at the beginning of my scientific career, instead of at the end of it, as I am now, I might perhaps choose no other field of study—in spite of its difficulties.

F.W.H. Myers—The Dissident View

One of Freud's contemporaries, F.W.H. Myers, may have been the first scholar in England to draw attention to the work of Freud and Breuer. He criticized it because he did not think hypnosis should be limited to treatment of hysteria, but saw other healthy aspects of consciousness affected by hypnosis. Myers felt they confined their work to a view of the subconscious as a repository for disease, but he believed it was the "healing principle" that their patients contacted through hypnosis, which then acted on the hysterical symptoms.

Since Freud and Breuer and Myers were all studying hypnotic phenomena at the same time, why are Freud and Breuer famous for their work and Myers virtually unknown? Freud and Breuer used hypnosis to relieve hysterical symptoms. Once a useful purpose for hypnosis was found, it was taken out of the realm of the occult and accepted as real and valuable.

Myers, on the other hand, wanted to understand how hypnosis works in relation to subliminal consciousness and what hypnotic phenomena suggested about our total selves. He proposed an extremely difficult project—that's not a popular thing to do. Also, the sensationalism of Freud's theories on sexuality took center stage and obscured Myers, who was a Cambridge-educated classical scholar and poet—not a psychoanalyst.

Myers' book, *Human Personality and Its Survival of Bodily Death*,[3] was published in 1903 and reissued several times. An abridged version appeared in 1907, so Myers' psychological theories have been before the public for over 75 years. This is quite an achievement for a psychology textbook.

Myers and others who founded the first Society for Psychical Research were dissatisfied and depressed by the view of humans as automatons. They specialized in the investigation of phenomena that had been neglected by orthodox science and that promised to throw more light on the truth of human nature. They studied psychological phenomena such as multiple personalities, hysteria, dreams and hallucinations, as well as the curious phenomena of "spiritualism," a tradition that sought answers about life beyond the body. Sigmund Freud and Swiss psychoanalyst Carl G. Jung were both members of the Society at one time, along with Nobel-Prize-winning physicists, statesmen, educators, and some of the finest minds of the era. The efforts begun in 1882 by the Society for Psychical Research continue today, over 100 years later.

In the early days, the work of the Society was suppressed in every way possible, short of disbandment. But who could disband such a group of dignitaries? However, as Freud's more sensational ideas found more and more favor, psychic research became less and less acceptable. Myers' beliefs that a "universal" subliminal self animates all personalities, that it is the source of all consciousness, that it transcends time and space, and that an individual might attain an experience of total consciousness were considered heretical.

As an analogy of consciousness, Myers used the example of the electromagnetic spectrum. Ordinary consciousness can be compared to the visible spectrum. Below the physiological limit are motor elements. While these aspects seem involuntary, hypnosis, biofeedback, and autosuggestion all indicate that even these elements can be modified, for example, in behavior modification or aversive conditioning. Above the psychological limit are the inspirations of genius, prodigies, creative dreams, and ESP abilities. Myers regarded the extraordinary aspects of mind as evidence of one's spirituality, not one's irrationality.

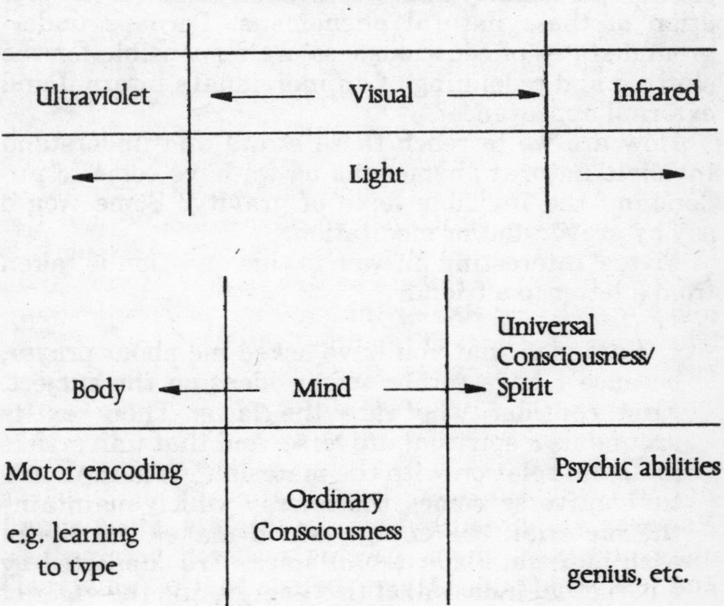

He thought consciousness was stratified, as is the Earth itself. We have soil on top of clay, sandstone, limestone, granite, and so forth, to the iron core. Yet, one substance is not superior to any other, and all are necessary. Myers wondered if there were streams of consciousness structured much like the Earth's stratifications. Ordinary consciousness is essential for common daily experience but need not be considered the only stratum of consciousness available for human experience.

For example, there are underground streams that may bubble up and change not only the shape of the underground terrain, but also the shape of the earth's surface. Therefore, such phenomena as geysers, volcanoes, and earthquakes rise out of various geothermal conditions. Perhaps experiencing the transformation of one's personality and/or behavior parallels the creation of these natural phenomena. Perhaps underground states of consciousness are responsible for the shifting and redefining of an individual's internal and external appearance?

How are we to reach these strata and understand invisible natural phenomena as we have come to understand the invisible force of gravity? Some would say by prayer and/or meditation.

Myers' interesting answer to this question is taken from a letter to a friend:

> I am glad that you have asked me about prayer, because I have rather strong ideas on the subject. First consider what are the facts. There exists around us a spiritual universe, and that universe is in actual relation with the material. From the spiritual universe comes the energy which maintains the material; the energy which makes the life of each individual spirit. Our spirits are supported by a perpetual indrawal of this energy, and the vigor of our absorption of material nutriment changes from hour to hour.

I call these "facts" because I think that some scheme of this kind is the only one consistent with our actual evidence: too complex to summarize here. How, then, should we *act* on these facts? Plainly we must endeavor to draw in as much spiritual life as possible, and we must place our minds in any attitude which experience shows to be favorable to such indrawal. *Prayer* is the general name for that attitude of open and earnest expectancy. If we then ask to *whom* to pray, the answers (strangely enough) must be that *that* does not much matter. The prayer is not indeed a purely subjective thing;—it means a real increase in intensity of absorption of spiritual power or grace;—but we do not know enough of what takes place in the spiritual world to know how the prayer operates;—*who* is cognizant of it, or through what channel the grace is given.

Myers suspected that our potential is unlimited. He saw sensory abilities as the result of natural selection for effective daily functioning. He theorized that humanity struggled for deliverance from illusion to spiritual unity in the impersonal All, and that this was an evolutionary process. "In our search for laws relating to the unseen world we must beware of setting our sights too high at first," he said. "... We must learn first not what we are most eager to learn, but what fits on best to what we know already."

There doesn't seem to be much discussion of spiritual evolution in the 20th-century media or educational institutions. By and large, people today are tired, frustrated, depressed, and spiritually bankrupt —and they don't know why. When their confusion becomes truly pronounced, it deprives them of the fun they had as children, and they more or less stop asking important questions. Their minds are put on hold as they work for a living, trying their best just to get along. They don't want to rock the boat, or think beyond the sophisticated and effective brainwashing they have received in their schooling—all based on the theories of materialistic psychologists, mechanistic biologists, and one-dimensional philosophers.

Lost in Material Space

When we ask such questions as, Why are we here? and What is the meaning of life? we pay more credence to the facts we learned in school than to our own spiritual or ecstatic experiences, which were usually minimized or discredited by those around us. The "facts," however, rarely satisfy our deepest longings, and they leave us with a terrible sense of emptiness and aloneness. We have been told we are highly complex machines and much evidence has been provided to prove that this is so. But how can a machine—no matter how complex—steadily hold a conviction that, somehow or other, it is more than a machine?

Biologist and philosopher Rupert Sheldrake wrote, "Any new theory capable of extending or going beyond the mechanistic theory will have to do more than assert that life involves qualities or factors at present unrecognized by the physical sciences: It will have to say what sorts of things these qualities or factors are, how they work, and what relationship they have to known physicochemical processes."[4] He is studying the resonances of morphogenetic fields in the attempt to develop a theory of behavioral evolution.

Morphogenetic fields are like the blueprints of a house. The blueprints guide the construction, but energy must be expended to get the actual task accomplished or no house will be built. Morphogenetic fields are nonenergetic but essential to the final outcome.

The original experiment on which this type of thinking is based was begun by William McDougall at

Harvard in 1920. White rats (Wistar strain) were put in a tank of water. Their task was to learn that an unilluminated gangway would lead them out of the water. If they swam to an illuminated gangway and started up, they received an electrical shock. Once a rat "got it," and discovered that the dim gangway was the way out, succeeding animals would generally not make the error of taking the bright gangway. This experiment was continued for 32 rat generations, and took 15 years to complete. It seems that once information is internalized—once a morphogenetic field is established—it is passed on through morphic resonance to other members of the species.

More Than Mere Bodies

In physical evolution, self-preservation is the goal; in conscious evolution, self-knowledge and self-actualization are the goals. Our consciousness selects what we pay attention to in our environment. For instance, you will probably attend to the voice of one who calls to you, but not necessarily to the buzzing of a fly in the room once you have heard it. What comes to consciousness, and what doesn't, may have originally been determined by some process of natural selection. Many things may claim our attention today that our ancestors in no way could have conceived.

It has been scientifically established that humans have extrasensory abilities, including telepathy (direct mind-to-mind communication), precognition (knowledge of the future), clairvoyance (information about distant objects and events), and psychokinesis, or PK (the ability of mind to manipulate matter). One-tenth of the available scientific data collected on these abilities for the past hundred years would be sufficient to cause scientists to accept any other phenomena. Margaret Mead said, in defense of the Parapsychological Association when it was admitted into membership in the American Association for the Advancement of Science in 1969, "The whole history of scientific advancement is full of scientists investigating phenomena that the establishment did not believe were there."

It's not that the scientific community is incapable of understanding the nature of human experience. It seems more likely that scientists are either complacent, apathetic, or afraid of the idea that human beings are more than mere bodies—which is what physical scientists, biologists, and behaviorists, among others, would like us to believe. Many of the world's religions chastise us for being sinners "bound" to the flesh, instead of teaching us that we are spiritual beings forever free in the wonders of nature. We are told that we must succumb to matter, to things as they are, rather than that we can operate through the unchanging laws of nature to exercise our God-given dominion over matter. It is not to the advantage of greedy power seekers that we should identify ourselves as free, invisible, creative beings. It seems impossible to most people to believe that we can change our outlook on life and create whatever we choose as we gain accurate knowledge of ourselves, our basic nature, our needs, purposes, and goals. In Western society it's as if the *life of the being* is considered less valuable and relevant than the *life of the body.* The value and importance of spiritual and intuitive experiences are underestimated in our verbally and sensory-dominated society.

Integrating the Totality of Human Experience

A positive approach to understanding human experience and evolution would be, first, to recognize our vast potential as multidimensional beings, and then, to emphasize cultural values that would nurture and harness these powerful energies with extreme care. At present, the largest political powers in the world are involved in daily death and destruction, pouring billions of dollars into the proliferation of military and nuclear hardware. Perhaps, as more people look inward for solutions to problems, a worldwide change in consciousness can occur and prevent global tragedy.

We can no longer assume that aggressive, individualistic behavior is the only model that works. Significantly, it has been men, not women, who have controlled each culture's military activities in the past and present. And yet, today, we see women imitating men in the marketplace and political arena.

However, the next evolutionary step does not seem to be for women to imitate the male model of aggression and dominance, but for men to integrate their own intuitive and nurturing abilities, along with the capacity for relationship that women have long mastered. Social institutions, which are currently controlled by men, do not reflect such feminine values. When men as well as women learn to act from intuition as well as logic, social changes reflecting the totality of human experiences will occur, resulting in a better life for the entire human race. An example of this may be seen in Centers of Concern created by South African women to try to stem another bloody male revolution there. Women try to save life everywhere—nowhere is it more dramatically presented than in the plight of South African society.

Still, a woman is free to exercise her intuition, even though she may be criticized and misunderstood. A man may feel more inhibited about discussing intuitive experiences seriously. One reason is that he may be less able to convert intuitive thought into language. Physiologically, women seem to have more facility for transferring right brain (intuitive) data into left brain (logical) speech and vice versa. A personal revolution occurs once the value of intuition is experienced and it is blended into logical actions. A new freedom can be experienced as we take responsibility for our own lives and realize our connectedness to the world and to each other.

It may be necessary to shed some of our most cherished conceptions, preconceptions, and sophistication in order to approach revolutionary ideas about human consciousness unhampered by feelings of superiority, prejudice, and fixed ideas about time and space. As we reorder our assumptions, a whole branch of knowledge may be established concerning our conscious evolution and emerging abilities.

Parapsychology is currently the science with the most information on our expanded human abilities. However, that information is not being offered to people widely enough at the moment to aid in their increased understanding and personal evolution. If another branch of knowledge, such as conscious evolutionary research and theory, were established and communicated to people in a way they could understand and use, this would automatically expand our knowledge base and move us forward. Remember, conscious evolution—in terms of expanded knowledge, rather than physical survival—is the goal of evolution today.

Chapter 1
End Notes

[1]Stuart Litvak & A. Wayne Senzee, "The Evolving Brain (Never Mind Darwin)," *New Realities* (Sept./Oct. 1986), pp. 26–32.

[2]William James, *Varieties of Religious Experience*. New York: New American Library, 1958, p. 354.

[3]F.W.H.Myers, *Human Personality and Its Survival of Bodily Death* (2 vols.). New York: Arno Press, 1975 (Original work published 1903).

[4]Rupert Sheldrake, *A New Science of Life*. Los Angeles: Tarcher, 1981, p. 11.

Chapter II

EVOLUTION OF CONSCIOUSNESS

There are those who understand that we are now engaged in the process of rapidly evolving consciousness. There are others who think we are mere water vessels. As people shift from self-consciousness to "cosmic consciousness," as R. M. Bucke called it in his classic work of the same name, or "direct knowing" as I choose to view it, there is bound to be a period of confusion. Groups are forming around the world to assist people who are emerging into new levels of expanded human awareness.

Groups such as Silva Mind Control, Spiritual Frontiers Fellowship, Science of Mind, and many other organizations tend to tell individuals they are not unique but not alone in their quests, not mentally ill, and that there is help and understanding available from those who are already learning to live with these different concepts of reality. These dedicated groups are very important in this stage of human evolution. They help to allay the inevitable feelings of fear and separateness that often accompany experiences of expanded consciousness.

One such group was originally known as the Spiritual Emergency Network (SEN), but when they saw the numbers of people needing information while in the process of emerging spiritually, they changed their name to Spiritual Emergence Network.

These groups share the understanding that expanded human consciousness is based on the knowledge that each of us is a whole being made up of body, mind, and spirit, and this, in turn, gives us further knowledge and edification of the meaning and purpose of our existence. The rapid expansion of such organizations is an indication that we are on the brink of an evolutionary leap in consciousness that is going to change the way we think and act toward one another.

Breakthrough to the Invisible

It is this breakthrough in consciousness that is causing so many of us to reorder our assumptions about life. We are shifting our perceptions, correcting misperceptions, questioning authority, and getting rid of illusions. Society has taught us our limits—"You can't do this . . . you can't do that." But now it is time to discard misconceptions based on false assumptions that have resulted in feelings of pain and separation.

As visionary Buckminster Fuller suggested, we have been educated, and the word "educate" means to be led out of ignorance. Now our need is for "introcation" or "inducation," to be led into new awarenesses. Fuller believed that *the real crisis from which we are suffering is our inability to deal with invisible reality.*

For example, if a conglomerate cannot run an energy source (solar, wind, etc.) through a wire or pipe, regulate it, and charge for it, they do not grant that source of energy its reality, and they tell the public we have an energy crisis or lack of energy. This sort of idea gets accepted by the masses, fear sets in, and the price goes up. We don't know how to deal with invisible reality. We can see the telephone wires but not the conversations—the invisible reality—taking place inside them.

Did you ever think of the telephone in terms of mental telepathy? The first telephone patent was issued in America in 1876. Around 1882, psychic researchers in England began to try to discover how telepathy operates. Parapsychologists are still trying to identify the channels of paranormal communication. But Ma Bell just keeps making it easier to transmit thoughts around the globe and out into space. Sometimes I think the parapsychologists have missed the technological advances in thought transference. Of course, it is still more exciting to think of communication without technology until you realize that the word "technology" can be defined as "the totality of the means employed to provide objects necessary for human sustenance and comfort." Keep in mind that technology is designed to supply us with our needs, as you read about the need-based theories of ESP in later chapters. If there is a channel of extrasensory communication, why not an instrument?

Telepathy has been scientifically verified. When two people are involved in a telepathic communication, one person is described as a "sender," and the other as a "receiver." Although the telephone makes the as yet unreliable ability of telepathy unnecessary in most cases, the words used to describe the function of telepathy are similar to those used for the telephone. For example, you pick up a "receiver" to get a message from the caller. Was the telephone invented to facilitate our telepathic abilities, which were weak and unreliable?

Think of the complexity of human speech, how one uses the larynx to break the steady air stream from the lungs into a series of puffs that produce audible sounds. When using the phone, you breathe these puffs of air into a sort of microphone—the sending part of the receiver. The sound is then converted into electrical impulses for transmission by wire, then reconverted to sound at the other end and the other person knows what you are thinking and trying to communicate to them.

We are surrounded by such miracles. It all began with the telegraph—sending dots and dashes of electrical impulses across the ocean to keep up with minute-to-minute price changes on imports and exports. Now we can use words and talk about anything we choose. Telegraph, telephone, radio, television—all the media that fill our lives today have emerged to enable us to form connections and facilitate communications so that we all may gain more knowledge and evolve.

Television has an important role to play in our conscious evolutionary process and can impart quality knowledge through its presentations. For instance, they could use more personal, intimate themes in commercials rather than sex and one-upmanship. AT&T's "Reach out and touch someone" is an example of a commercial that relates to our need for connectedness, with the company telling us that they want to help facilitate our meeting that need. One can respect this approach to advertising.

McDonald's commercials speak to family needs and self-esteem. They tell their customers they are worth it with their "You deserve a break today" ads. This is an attempt to raise self-esteem, but much more could be done. People are sometimes affected by this kind of commercial. I saw a businessman rushing to catch a subway and the doors closed right in front of him. He was frustrated and obviously had to get to his destination immediately. All at once the conductor started singing over the intercom, "You deserve a break today," opened the subway doors, and let the man enter. Everyone in the car enjoyed the kindness, and it was one of my more pleasant New York City subway rides.

There is still too much emphasis on sex role stereotypes for the sale of products. Macho men drink beer and very feminine women color their hair and put on false fingernails. This emphasis on sex to sell everything from jeans to lipstick does nothing to raise consciousness. Because of their short, fast viewing time, commercials affect the viewers' subconscious. They could be used for enhancing how people feel about themselves, as beings rather than just bodies. Looking good is important, but it is shortsighted as a goal.

The labeling of products also takes on interesting dimensions when viewed in this light. We have cars on the market today named Accord and Valiant. Clearly, the automobile industry's sales force is aware of our need for connectedness and strong character, and chooses these names to make us think that by owning these cars we will be filling those needs at some level. Drug labels use this same technique. For instance, two of the highest selling drugs on the market are Librium and Valium. The connotation is that you will be strong and free if you take these substances. Ironically, the concepts of liberty and value have been turned into consumer products that create dependency rather than freedom. At least the advertisers got one thing right—they have identified what we want and need on a nonphysical level. They attempt to meet that need through material and physical means. As more and more people pick up on what is being transmitted through these messages, they may begin to seek the source within them that offers the strength, freedom, and connectedness they desire.

Bucke wrote his famous work, *Cosmic Consciousness,* in 1901.[1] Since then the process of conscious evolution has been speeded up tremendously. With over five billion of us on the planet now, we are seeking knowledge in ever-expanding ways. After all, we have only been writing and talking to each other over distance for a few hundred years. Now, with communication being facilitated to the point of live TV pictures from any place on the planet and far out into space, it is through our language and understanding of one another's experience that we are evolving.

We are joining hands personally around the world through programs for exchange students and sponsored children. Americans learn firsthand about another culture by living in other countries, while students from other countries are living with Americans and learning about our culture. It will be more difficult to view people from other countries as dehumanized, faceless enemies once we can get to know and love and learn from them.

Many Americans are sponsoring children who live in foreign countries. In sponsored-children programs, one may communicate with a child for years by mail and get to know and genuinely care for that person. If war was to break out in the vicinity of one's sponsored child, it would not just be something happening "over there," we would be concerned for our little friend's safety. War will become more and more unacceptable as we embrace each other around the globe with the feeling of family. Through these worldwide programs involving children and young people, we may be led out of strife into international love and respect. Becoming "world people" is a goal of conscious evolution.

These programs constitute one hope for unifying the people of this planet. However, there is another possibility that may sound strange, but seems fairly logical. UFO sightings have been increasing steadily, and people now report more actual contact with aliens than ever before. There are many people on this planet who believe they have had direct contact with beings from another part of the universe or beyond. If it were to become a known fact that we are in contact with extraterrestrials, this could have a tremendous impact on our evolutionary process. If extraterrestrials can come here in physical form and communicate with us, they would clearly be ahead of us in knowledge and technology and therefore evolved in these terms. Being in communication with them could give us a visible evolutionary goal. On the other hand, they might possibly be considered yet another competitive group. An even worse danger is that aliens could become yet another war target, which we seem to be training for now with our video games. The good that could come out of extraterrestrial contact would be the collapse of the walls of separateness created by nationalism, racism, and false superiority as we discover we are Earthlings and that there are other intelligent life forms. I believe that eventually something will trigger us into identifying ourselves as planetary citizens—if we don't destroy the planet first. By way of practice, let's see how another culture views evolution.

Evolutionary Theory—East Vs. West

The Hindu theory of evolution is quite different from our Western theories. They believe the true secret of evolution is the manifestation of the perfection that is already within every being; that this perfection has somehow been blocked, and the underlying surging spirit beneath it is struggling to express itself. They believe that within each of us there is a potential god, kept in by the locks and bars of ignorance. When knowledge breaks these bars, the god becomes manifest through the person. This is not to suggest that the perfection we aim for is a static condition. There is no reason to assume that perfection excludes change. One's idea of perfection can change. You can see a perfect sunset, but it does not mean you will never see another perfect one, even though it won't be the same sunset.

Our civilization offers us the possibility of material gain, but not necessarily spiritual satisfaction. Although there may be gratification in the possession of wealth and consumer items, people also crave knowledge of what life is all about and why we are here. What is our purpose, as a group and individually? These are the ideas and questions we earnestly need to discuss if we are going to prevent planetary catastrophe. If those who are trying to discuss these issues are ridiculed or not taken seriously by those who have influence through media, then all of us are being held back in ignorance by a minority.

Let's get the facts on the table, then together we can decide what is useful and what is not. Nightly viewings of multiple deaths and car chases on television surely cannot be that useful to our society at this crucial stage of our evolution. Do we believe that televising the ravages of deceit and dishonesty in minute detail can possibly uplift anyone's spirit or inspire a noble deed?

Of course we are capable of every perverse action from deceit to murder. But we are also capable of magnanimous acts of love, compassion, and sharing. Media continually offer us perverse acts (physical, emotional, or mental) as situations in which one person has power over another. If a person has a gun pointed at you, it is clear who has the power. But, examine your own life and remember times when you felt powerful. Wasn't it on occasions when you knew you were truly alive; when you felt strong in body and mind; when your heart was filled with joy? It is at times like these that you know the power of your being. You do not have to take power from anyone, hold power over anyone, beg, borrow or steal power—it is all yours just like the air you breathe. You can become aware of this power anytime you turn to it in honesty—in humility, gratitude, sincerity.

Reordering Assumptions

In order to realize our power, we may have to reorder our assumptions. Our self-limitations are often based on assumptions deriving from theories that have never been proved. For instance, the first thing a person usually asks on seeing a new baby is: "Is it a boy or a girl?" Once this information is obtained, they can begin to talk to the child. The reason people talk to boys differently from girls is based on a certain set of assumptions. People generally talk more directly to boys, thereby granting them more humanness. The tone of their voices when talking to girls is often something akin to the way they talk to pets rather than peers. It seems to be assumed that girls won't appreciate directness, but boys will.

Differing roles begin to be imposed on the sexes at first human contact. We assume roles based on this kind of conditioning. We repress or suppress behavior that would not be appropriate to the roles we have assumed. Those who step outside prescribed roles to be whoever or whatever they feel themselves to be at that moment usually face opposition, although they might be called originals or individuals by some. Most people are intimidated by those who refuse rigid roles and often label them rebels, troublemakers, nonconformists, or snobs. Those who feel limited or trapped by conventional roles are usually jealous or afraid of the freedom of the individual. Since the role players are usually in the majority, rules and regulations are set up that label them "normal." Labels and categories are then created to try to "capture" the free spirit.

I am not denying the existence of genuine mental illness, but sometimes if individuals experience life fully, from ecstasy to agony, with no shame at being seen feeling and expressing their emotions, the majority, represented in this case by the psychological/psychiatric community, might choose to label them manic-depressive and give them drugs or shock treatments to "level out their moods." If the person is getting in touch with psi abilities and expanded consciousness, he or she may be branded a schizophrenic, and in addition to the above treatments face imprisonment ("institutionalization" is the nice word). If individuals are alert and aware of the hazards on this planet, they are often called paranoid by those in denial of such hazards.

When you validate a personal ESP experience it may be like the feeling you get when you hit the jackpot in Las Vegas. Parapsychologists didn't start testing for ESP ability with cards and dice for no reason. Be aware that this winning feeling can be addictive. Can you handle it? If not, you may lose freedom rather than obtaining more freedom.

Psychiatric View of Appropriate Behavior

At this point in time, the American Psychiatric Association probably views Shirley MacLaine's paranormal experiences as symptomatic of mental disorder. Their bible is *DSM-3* (the *Diagnostic and Statistical Manual, Third Edition*). This is the book that defines and determines the "appropriate" way to experience life—according to some. If you venture outside its limits into such experiences as clairvoyance, telepathy, precognition, or out-of-body explorations, you are deemed mentally deranged. I love the expression "mental disorders." Who is it that orders my mental experiences? Who is to say whether I can go beyond "normal" societal limits in my thinking—or that I am out of order? Who has the right to censor human experience?

I'm for personal freedom, and I think each of us is entitled to experience the universe any way we choose to. Although we are not entitled to force that experience on any one else, or to harm others by exercising our freedom, we are entitled to have any transpersonal experience we may have and to define it the way we choose. *It is our experience as we know it that is the truth of our being.*

Psychophobia and the "Norm" Enforcers

Psychiatrist and author R. D. Laing addresses this problem by saying, "People are frightened of the possibilities of their own minds. I call this *psychophobia.* There's a psychophobic trend in our culture that is particularly common among people who are motivated by fear of experiential anarchy. [Anarchy: where each one is entitled to experience the universe his or her own way.] And these people are the ones who dedicate themselves to policing other people's experiences and minds."[2]

Because of such fears, most of us seldom try to understand these types of experiences. We try to neutralize or negate them. We strive to make behavior conform to an invisible norm, rather than attempting to understand the wide range of human behavior. The family agrees whatever the "doctor" says is best, based on an assumption that doctors know. These medical enforcers of the "norm" are seldom interested in expanded states of awareness. Such norm enforcers do know behaviorist theory, however, and therefore believe that any behavior that cannot be controlled or regulated must be "wrong."

Often those who are fully alert and aware, in touch with psi abilities, and experiencing life enthusiastically and vitally, are repeatedly warned to "calm down." Or admonished to fulfill their role, or to just get in line. This kind of social control, which is often carried out by members of our educational/psychological/psychiatric communities, is too often part of "business as usual." Such social control is felt to be necessary, however, in a society where a handful of the elite (the *Fortune* 500, for instance) run the country.

Religious organizations also take part in this social control and are often rewarded by donations from the elite for their good work. Political organizations certainly use social control and for a good reason. People stuck in prescribed roles are usually so bored with life they don't think much. They don't want to—it's all too confusing. All one has to do is decide on a political party (probably Dad's or Mom's) and let the party do all that thinking for you. All you have to do is follow their instructions as to whom and what you should vote for or against.

Your boss can control how you do your work. Sure, there are incentive awards, but don't get too innovative, especially in the direction of improved quality and lowered price.

Your spouse can control your behavior in the home. While most people don't want to give much attention to their own behavior, they are usually more than willing to exert as much control as possible over another person's behavior.

Your religious institution controls your perception and experience of spirituality. With all these prescribed behavioral guidelines, you are free to think about ballgames, clothes, cars, makeup, and sex. One day you may discover that you are stuck in the material world and realize that those who you are letting do the thinking can do anything they want to you. They *are* in control. They can even annihilate you and your planetary home.

Language and Evolution

In order to avoid such dire consequences, we need the desire to learn more about conscious evolution. One thing that separates human beings from every other life form is our aptitude for language. One aspect of our uniqueness is the possession of a brain that can generate grammar. It has been theorized for decades by psycholinguistic pioneer Noam Chomsky and others that the mechanism of language acquisition is an innate, biological, genetically determined property of human beings. Language is forever shifting and changing; new words are emerging, and old ones are passing out of use. We don't know for sure how language gets changed, by whom, or why.

Language could have been a special mutation among humans that won out through natural selection by supplying everyone with genes for language, or it could have come into existence as a latent property of all human brains at some point in the evolution of humanity. Imagine what it would be like if we discovered another latent property as powerful as language in our brains right now. Our lives could be as profoundly changed as it was when language first appeared. Such a discovery is possible, because we are human be-comings, living in a truly exciting time.

Children have a facility for languages that adults seldom possess. Bickerton, author of *Roots of Language*, confirms Chomsky's theory through a study of a language crisis that occurred in Hawaii around 1880. Thousands of people were brought to the islands to work. They spoke many different languages and were unable to communicate with one another. Surprisingly, within one generation a whole new language evolved among the people. Bickerton states that this new language could only have been constructed by children.

Language may continue to be used to mystify and

preserve power. Listen to most doctors, lawyers, or politicians, if you doubt that this is true. We can talk a subject to death or at least to extreme perversion—haven't we talked enough about sex yet? We can even talk the joy out of an experience. Nevertheless, we do need to talk about human experiences, especially those that affect the core of our being and all our future perceptions of what is real and significant. Reality is arrived at in a community by agreement. If everyone agrees they are unsafe, communication will be stifled and doors and windows will be locked and barred. We agree on our reality. However, such agreements can be altered.

Encoding Information into Memory

As important as language is, there are other ways of encoding information into memory. In most discussions of thinking and problem solving, as well as of ESP and the human information-processing system,[3] verbal and visual memory codes have been emphasized. There is a third type of memory code that preserves motor activity. It has been called an "enactive code"[4] or "motor program."[5] It will be necessary for us to understand skills, as well as visual and verbal images, if we are to develop a thorough investigation of the human information-processing system.

Motor memory codes are different from visual and verbal memory codes in the way they function, and this difference has tended to exclude them from the study of thinking. Motor memory codes require reduced involvement of attention in both their storage and performance. It is just this difference that may prove important in the relationship between motor memory codes and ESP functioning. If ESP operates along some specific information channel, it is reasonable to assume that it is "active" most of the time.

However, one may not always be consciously aware of the ESP channel activity. ESP may operate more frequently on an unconscious level, in the service of personal needs and self-preservation.

In cognitive psychology, the study of motor memory codes has been somewhat neglected. Right hemisphere brain functions (where intuition supposedly operates) were also largely ignored in physiological studies for the first fifty years. Neurologists primarily studied the left hemisphere, where damage could cause verbal impairment. Research on verbal retention is much more sophisticated methodologically than that on motor retention. In general, it appears that continuous motor responses (for instance, typing for an experienced typist) are retained much better than verbal responses, whereas discrete motor responses (one's first typing lesson) show a similar retention to verbal responses. Jack Adams (1967) makes a clear distinction between motor and verbal learning:

> Motor behavior is bodily movement.... Speech is the motor behavior involved in the production of sounds, and it is comprised of lip, tongue, and jaw movements, and the muscular control of vocal cords.... Verbal learning, on the other hand, is the acquisition of new symbolic relations, not new motor movements.[6]

Methodological bias in research can create false impressions within society. As J. P. Guilford (1959) puts it:

> Verbal comprehension is undoubtedly a very important trait in a verbal civilization, but its relatively strong predictive power and its obvious role in education has often obscured the importance of other intellectual factors. The overemphasis upon it in testing and in education may

have led to serious neglect of other desirable qualities in the general population.[7]

In education, as well as research, verbal skills have been deemed more important and valuable than performance skills. Early on, school populations are separated into those who score high on verbal tests and those who score low. If the population were evaluated, taking performance tests into account, it might redress the bias in favor of the verbally oriented students by creating hands-on, how-to courses along with reading and writing assignments. Students could then be assigned to instruction from which they would be most apt to benefit, and universities might not exclude prospective students solely on the basis of low verbal aptitude. In personnel testing, multiple aptitude test batteries are given, which include nonverbal and performance skills. However, achievement batteries for college entrants do not take performance tasks into account. We need college graduates who can do, as well as say. A recent ruling by Federal Judge John M. Walker also states that Scholastic Aptitude Tests in general discriminate against women, minorities, and the poor. This is the first federal decision that addresses this issue (*Wall Street Journal*, 2/10/89, pB3).

Child-development researchers Jean Piaget and Jerome Bruner indicate that infants get initial information about their world by manipulating the objects they hold in their hands. This fundamental relationship between the child and its world exists as the perceptual experience emerges, followed by language. Because our understanding of ESP is considered still in its infancy, it may prove enlightening to try to find a way to examine these motor memory codes, which appear to be storehouses of our first sense data. ESP information could be stored there, too, which may be why it is rarely accessible to verbal description. This may also be why adults who can perform an ESP skill usually do not know how to do it consciously, or how to repeat it as controlled behavior, or how to explain the process verbally.

Human infants work steadily at motor learning from birth in a rather slow and laborious trial-and-error manner. If using our bodies is the ultimate psychokinetic effect—and it may well be, since a conscious decision almost always precedes behavior—one can see how long it takes to acquire minimal physical skills, such as newborns' abilities to raise their heads, coordinate eye movements, raise head and upper trunk together, and to reach out and grasp things. Learning to walk usually precedes the more difficult task of learning to articulate words.

PK can be thought of in this regard as mind moving matter. For instance, you may decide to raise your hand to catch a cab or answer a question. You are thinking about the result of raising your hand—you might get a ride or be considered smart. Your hand is already in the air and you didn't give one thought as to *how* to get it there. But, as an infant, you practiced years to perfect this now automatic signal that might get your needs met. No one gave you a book on "how to move your body." They suggested you could do it, helped you by showing you how they did it, and then you were on your own to practice at body coordination and effective movement.

Everyone must go through these learning processes, and although we take them for granted, using our bodies is probably one of the most difficult things we ever have to learn. If this truly is an act of psychokinesis, then I theorize that ESP phenomena are so massive, so widespread, that they too are taken for granted and thus go undefined, as opposed to the current idea that ESP operates at a minimal level and must be viewed through the microscope of stastistics.

Parapsychologist S. D. Kahn also views psi phenomena as such a natural experience of life that it is likely to go unnoticed. He says, "an alternative to our present concept of psi . . . is [one] which argues that psi represents a broad process through which individuals are linked in far more fundamental and perhaps presently unimagined ways than by the occasional sharing of unusual perception."[8]

He realizes that "the idea of mental action at a distance remains peculiarly offensive to the scientific mind," and suggests that what passes as scientific skepticism is often a more basic fear that has its roots in early childhood memory patterns. From the psychoanalytic viewpoint, while infantile beliefs of magical actions superseding time and space are repressed in adulthood, they are never entirely abandoned. When we are confronted with the possibility of their reality (as in the case of evidence for ESP), it can be extremely anxiety producing. One needs to be skeptical in analyzing the evidence, but this skepticism must not be allowed to become a barrier against changing long-held concepts of reality. We would know very little about the physical universe today had physicists not been skeptical yet willing to change their world view in light of new discoveries.

Dissociated states, such as hypnosis, dreams, and sensory deprivation (as in the Ganzfeld, a method of sensory deprivation often used in ESP experiments), have been shown to be psi-conducive states, i.e., a state of consciousness in which positive ESP results are more likely to occur. It seems that the less attention one pays to the body, the more ESP is facilitated. Frederick Bartlett stated, concerning the muscular part of the skilled operation: "the more efficient it is, the less is known about it."[9] British psychologist U. T. Place states the same idea in another way: ". . . we say frequently of someone whose skill is already well developed that his performance suffered because he paid too close attention to what he was doing."[10]

Michael Posner[11] tells us motor memory codes are

used in such activities as riding a bicycle, batting a ball, or typing without looking at the keyboard. Also, one may be able to arrive at a specific location by making correct turns in walking there, yet not be able to describe the route beforehand. These operations are not simple. They require complex coordination and "programming." One may try to show another how to perform a physical skill, but basically people must use their own bodies and learn for themselves through practice. However, once they are learned, motor skills do not require constant vigilance, and it is just this reduced involvement of attention in motor code storage and performance that makes it different from other memory coding and possibly more amenable for ESP processing.

It has usually been speculated that verbal and visual memory structures are involved in ESP processes, too. After many years of active investigation of memory and ESP—using word-pairs with high- and low-association words; symbol, digit, or word recall lists; story recall; and similar linguistic techniques—we know little more now than when we started. We know that ESP and memory are both affected by psychological factors such as mood, attitude, and attention. Parapsychologists believe that similar processing of information may be involved in both memory and ESP, and that we should continue in our attempts to understand memory-ESP interactions.

While I agree that memory-ESP research may hold great promise for understanding the ESP process, I believe that memory work must include motor memory codes as well as verbal and visual ones. This seems especially important for ESP because of the evidence that ESP can show itself by correct autonomic physiological responses, which are not brought to consciousness and cannot be verbalized.

Stefan Figar, a Czechoslovakian M.D. and neurophysiologist, is not now nor has ever been interested in psi research. However, he did make an accidental discovery in his work in *plethysmography* that he felt could be of use to parapsychologists.[12] The plethysmograph measures fluid volume in the finger and thus shows autonomic changes. This means that, like the GSR, it is a measure of mental and emotional responses. A chart recorder plots these changes.

In Figar's experiments, he would connect a person's hand to the plethysmograph and obtain a straight baseline recording. Then he would give the person a card containing instructions to multiply two numbers mentally. As soon as the person began to do mental arithmetic, there was a rapid vasoconstriction in the finger. Figar began to observe something odd with several people. When he simply *thought* of giving the arithmetic card to the person, vasoconstriction would occur. It was as if the person read Figar's mind and knew the card was about to be presented.

Figar was so impressed with this finding that he placed two people on either side of a curtain to see if there were simultaneous vasoconstrictions in both of them when he presented arithmetic cards to only one of them at random times. It worked. As a result, he felt so strongly that some form of ESP communication was occurring that he offered his findings to psi researchers for a further look into the implications.

Parapsychologists have attempted to replicate this finding. E. D. Dean[13] has done the most extensive plethysmographic work in relation to ESP studies. When he found that mental arithmetic didn't work with his engineering college students, he tried names. He used five personal names submitted by the ESP sender, five from the receiver, five telephone book names, and five blank cards in a randomized deck. The receiver was hooked up to a plethysmograph and only knew that a sender was in another room looking at the names on the cards.

Twenty-second sending periods were marked on the

plethysmograms. Independent judges measured the vasoconstrictions in each period. Receivers produced significantly larger vasoconstrictions to the names they had submitted ($p=.012$), contrary to Dean's hypothesis that they would give larger reactions to senders' names, since senders could not discriminate receivers' names from telephone book names. Combinations of personally known names differed from telephone book names and blanks at a significance level of .004. Dean and C. B. Nash[14] then pooled their efforts and confirmed Dean's original findings.

In most ESP tests of the card-calling variety, results tend to decline over time due to boredom. Dean's experiments, however, held up over time and showed no decline effects. He felt this was because the ESP task was completely unconscious and therefore it was not necessary for the conscious mind to overcome boredom in order to continue to score in a consistent manner.

Is Cognitive Style Consistent with ESP Ability?

So, we see that language is not always the only factor in our evolving abilities—especially in the case of direct knowing.

In 1981, I used another approach to determine if one's regular preferred cognitive style (verbal or motor) would influence ESP results. The way one cognizes (knows) the world is the way it is for them and a certain style of interacting evolves from this knowing. Some people like to read, write, and talk—would they do better on a verbal ESP test? Others like to dance, paint, or do carpentry—would they score higher on a performance ESP test?

Forty women were given a battery of psychological tests in order to obtain nine scores each for performance abilities and verbal skills. In one test they filled out an interest inventory as to whether they liked certain tasks (some verbal; some performance). Each woman also completed one verbal and one performance clairvoyant ESP test. Tests included 72 verbal trials to name six different color targets in opaque envelopes, and 72 performance trials to place these target envelopes in the correct color-coded letter-type chutes in a wall.

The most significant correlation was found with the interest inventory self-rated verbal score—higher verbal scores were associated with higher verbal ESP and lower performance ESP. Self-rated performance scores were negatively correlated with verbal ESP and more positively correlated with performance ESP. It appears the women's own feelings about their cognitive styles extended to the realm of ESP, as good predictors.

Conceptual and Perceptual Thinking

Profound mysteries exist within human evolution. We have been educated here in the U.S. and other countries to be able to use and manipulate mental concepts. We are so used to conceptual thinking, it is probably difficult for most of us to imagine any other kind of thinking. However, before humans learned conceptual thinking, there was another way of thinking, and no doubt there are still those on Earth who operate the *other* way. Such individuals use perceptual thinking, which is limited to responding to perceived situations. This is called "stimulus-response thinking."

Conceptual thinking needs no external stimulus nor immediate response. Therefore, we can consider problems and solutions without being directly confronted with the problem physically. We can consider possibilities, visualize outcomes, and weigh mental alternatives and their consequences. We can do all this without taking any other action than thinking. Those of us who can think conceptually can also think perceptually; however, perceptual thinkers have to be taught concept formation.

Mind is dependent on speech for conceptual thought. Speech, as a form of communication, has been crucial to our conscious evolution. It is believed the grunts and chatterings of animals and early humans were expressions of mood that may or may not have been heard by others. It is possible these expressions evolved into a means of communication, demanding a hearer, and from here speech emerged. We can see the evolution of language in an infant who cries or goos in an attempt possibly to get milk or affection. The expressions "da-da" or "ma-ma" may be even more rewarding, and soon words begin to form and sentences are constructed. Language seems essential for conceptual thought, but it is still uncertain which came first. For instance, one could conceptualize in mental pictures without words and then communicate those ideas through hieroglyphics.

It is common to think of the mind in individual terms, i.e., your mind or my mind. In fact, there is evidence to support the theory that the mind is not confined to the body and brain with which it is associated. Expressions of one's mood, whether animal or human, can be communicated through noises, scents, color change, posture, and other forms of nonverbal communication. In our daily lives we are familiar with the many ways human beings communicate our moods to one another.

There are also indications of group mood in nature, for instance, in migrating birds, schooling fish, stampeding cattle, and mob reactions. Mind appears as a group phenomenon in these cases, and whatever mood is communicated or felt within the group causes the whole group to react similarly and simultaneously. It is possible to conceive that the stage of mental evolution that preceded self-consciousness was group consciousness. One only wonders how the first self-conscious individuals were treated in the group. Were they feared, revered, or just "run out of town"?

If we can consider that group consciousness evolved into self-consciousness, we may be able to hypothesize our next stage of evolution. R. M. Bucke believes this will be cosmic consciousness, in which we will not only be concerned with ourselves as individuals but be able to see ourselves as a valuable part of the cosmos. One revolutionary method of opening up cosmic consciousness is to move to the center of a group, then move to the edge and contemplate it, and then begin to see the group as merely a part of the grand scheme, or possibly a part that is suppressing the larger idea. We hear a lot of talk today about planetary consciousness, or what Buckminster Fuller called the "global village." We also hear of universal consciousness. But few seem to acknowledge that, despite its vastness, we inhabit only one universe of many. Bucke's cosmic consciousness is akin to our modern notion of universal consciousness.

This universe may be full of life struggling to evolve even though we haven't detected it yet. In the early stages of human evolution, a being is mainly concerned about conquering its environment, overcoming enemies, and assuring itself of food. But sooner or later, a point comes where evolution progresses beyond this stage, and we can turn our attention inward, to the pleasures of mind. We are at this stage of evolution now. Once we understand that our minds are realms where God's will is revealed and fulfilled, life will become a great adventure into unexplored territories. We will then know that we have crossed the borderline that divides an animal from the divine.

While evolution, in terms of survival, has been integral to life as we know it, today conscious evolution

—seeking for knowledge—has become an integral part of daily life. We are now able to see and record conscious evolution as a process and, if we are willing, we can facilitate the process. For instance, we understand self-consciousness as self-awareness and an essential step toward self-knowledge. The human species advances as it breaks down or otherwise removes barriers that reduce communication between our conscious and unconscious minds. As we move toward expanded self-knowledge, we still know that we are individuals, but we begin to grasp how totally connected everything is and the vast potential available to all of us.

The Role of Communication Systems

Up until the 16th century, conscious evolution dealt with self-awareness. After that time the tempo of mental evolution increased, and it has continued to speed up as we move into the realms of self-knowledge and self-actualization. Conscious evolution accelerated in large part due to our ever-expanding networks of communication. For instance, while printing has become the main vehicle for the conveyance of ideas, we've only had the technology for five hundred years. Before that time ideas were handed down through oral tradition or the laborious copying of hand-written manuscripts, which were only available to a select few. The invention of the printing press led to the distribution of knowledge to the masses, and those who had had no reason to learn to read became curious. That curiosity led to learning how to read, which then exposed individuals to so many new ideas that an even more insatiable curiosity for knowledge and information arose in the minds of many. This produced a profound social change because prior to the invention of the printed word, knowledge had been available only to those in power.

Several more centuries were to pass before the invention of the wire telegraph, the first practical long-range communications system. The first transcontinental telegraph message was sent in 1861. Bell's first telephone was introduced in 1876. Marconi sent the first transatlantic wireless message in 1901, and this was a first indication of the long-range possibilities of radio communications and the use of electromagnetic radiation to send signals through space. By 1922, we had sight with sound in the first motion pictures, and by 1939 some commercial television sets were in production.

Color TV was introduced in the U.S. in 1954. Having had access to this powerful medium of communication for less than 50 years, it is not surprising that we do not yet know how to use it to its best advantage as a tool to awaken people to their potential for self-actualization. Even in our ignorance, TV still creates an enormous impact on people's lives in more ways than simply getting them to buy a certain car, detergent, or wine cooler.

From the telegraph to television, electricity had been the medium used to convey information through space or by wire. In the 1970s, however, a new way of communicating was found—not by electricity but by light beam. This communications system, known as fiber optics, transmits light frequencies in glass fibers that can carry 10,000 times more information than electrical signals on copper wires, and 100 times more information than radio-frequency signals on coaxial cables. Thousands more access channels may be added for our selection, and these fiber optic light waves will conceivably be able to convey almost every type of program, information, and service we need into homes on demand.

The first communications satellite (Telstar) was

placed in orbit in July 1962. It reflected signals from Andover, Maine, to another ground station for approximately 16 minutes during each orbit. No more cables were needed and we didn't have to depend on the rather unreliable ionized (electrically charged) layers in the atmosphere to reflect radio signals. Satellites today can amplify signals they receive from one ground station and retransmit them to other stations as continuous television broadcasts. There are now hundreds of ground stations in operation around the world, and current technology allows for approximately 180 satellites in orbit. Cities and nations all over the planet are being linked together by use of these satellites.

The current technological revolution is mind boggling. Computers are becoming more sophisticated every day. Messages are now being transmitted in nanoseconds (1 billionth of a second). In terms of distance to a satellite, a nanosecond might be perceived as light traveling approximately six inches, as compared to the speed of light, which moves 186,000 miles in one second. We still need a lot of nanoseconds to get our messages 22,300 miles to a satellite. Now, there is talk of using "picoseconds" (which might be perceived as the size of one pepper flake). A picosecond is a 10,000th of a billionth of a second, or a quadrillionth of a second. If your mind isn't blown by this idea, wait until you start to see what happens to our everyday lives when we have access to superconductivity and nuclear fusion. There are already trains in Japan that "levitate" to reduce track friction and thus increase speed.

Evolution as Trial and Error

Evolution is a trial and error process.

There have always been warring tribes, but the

concept of nationalism first appeared in the 19th century. We all know how this one concept affects our thinking, the limits it sets, the barriers it erects against others, the animosities it nurtures, and the way people cling to it as a crutch. However, nationalism may be an experiment of evolution that failed, and satellite communications may be just the link we need to become planetary people. The world is growing smaller in our consciousness, and we have already seen live television pictures from our Moon and other planets in our solar system. If an alien intelligence is detected through radio telescopes and communications refinements, I believe it will strengthen this link between Earth inhabitants.

Fifty years ago these technological breakthroughs would have been considered science fiction. Today, they are our reality. It is impossible to imagine the advances of the next fifty years at the rate we are going. It is important to get a proper perspective on our evolutionary position.

Mind Vs. Matter

The most damaging assumption we may have been suffering from so far in our evolution could well be that mind and matter are two different entities. Philosopher John Roddam writes:

> Galileo made the distinction between mind and matter purely as an analytical convenience. His work on matter was arrested by the Church and never completed; Part II, "mind," was never written. This fatal dichotomy survived at first because the Church was powerful enough to forbid inquiry. The division was perpetuated, almost certainly for the same reason, in Cartesian philosophy. The distinction became traditional. It

> thus came about that physics was studied and psychology was not. The mind became taboo as a subject of inquiry. The Church kept the meat of the mind for itself and threw the bone of matter to the lay dog. Man became an observer who dispassionately dissected the Universe but who never turned his gaze inwards. The eye can see all things except the observer.
>
> Until about a hundred years ago, . . . the Universe was regarded as a machine. . . . God was the machine-minder.[15]

This mechanical theory of the universe couldn't be scientifically verified and seemed to belittle God, so it was then assumed that God functioned within the machine of creation through a chosen agent—human beings.

We had already been told by Darwin that our physical bodies evolved from apes. It is possible that we chose not to find out where the mind came from at this point, as it might be too degrading. All ideas about where mind originated were repressed into our unconscious. Freud taught us to acknowledge the existence of the unconscious mind, which allowed us to begin to realize what clues lie there for our evolutionary process. It is only as we begin to realize there is something we don't know, that we can begin to know it. If we don't know we don't know, we will never know. Assumptions cannot be reordered without taking the uncomfortable position of acknowledging our unknowingness.

Psychic Ingo Swann, who wrote *Natural ESP*, emphasized the importance of getting rid of the "analytical overlay,"[16] so that he could pick up the ESP signal out of the noise of mind. This means you have to lay aside everything you thought you knew about a subject in order to view it in its purest sense. As John Roddam wrote,

> It is necessary to slough off layers of analytical thinking and translate one's mind back to a stage of prehistory, buried for the most part deep in the unconscious, before man was self-conscious, and before he ever considered appealing to reason; to a time before he theorized, and before he assumed or concluded that the law of causation underlay all sequences of events.[17]

"A centipede was happy quite, until a toad in fun, said 'Pray, which leg goes after which?', which threw its mind into such a pitch, it lay distracted in a ditch, considering how to run."

This story reflects the classification dichotomy that caused many minds to "fall in a ditch." Events began to be classified as either natural or supernatural probably as far back as prehistoric times. These two categories still stand today: Natural events are predictable and can be utilized and controlled; supernatural events happen unexpectedly, cannot be controlled, and are usually feared. To account for the supernatural, religion was invented. People created myths, which later were considered facts and therefore not open to analysis. Magical practices and rituals had probably been used prior to the creation of religion to ward off the harmful effects of the supernatural.

People did not always envision gods in human form. Anthropomorphism is not a "primitive" concept, but one initiated among civilized people. When people became self-conscious (aware of their individual uniqueness), they transferred that uniqueness to powers that previously represented the unknown.

In order to anthropomorphize god, it was necessary to have myths in which women became impregnated by spirit, or were at least allowed to conceive major religious figures against tremendous odds. For example, Isaac, John the Baptist, Jesus, Horus, Zarathustra, Buddha, Lao-Tzu, and Dionysus are all shown as part human, part god. Following this ancient pan-Earth tradition, Jesus was seen as the son of God, and the founder of one of the world's great religions. Many early religious traditions focused their practices on propitiating the gods to temper the brute forces of nature. However, over time, as the world's great religious traditions evolved, the emphasis shifted to a belief in a just and loving divine presence that permeated all living things and dwelled in the heart of each individual human being.

So, by degrees, the supreme being was brought down to Earth in human form. In the beginning, we had created a god to explain the inexplicable. But as our knowledge increased, we undermined the foundations of our creation. It is difficult, if not impossible, to maintain belief in a supreme being when the mysteries of God unfold to reveal natural, rather than supernatural, origins. It appears we had made god too small, for a supreme being cannot be contained in a human concept for long.

After centuries of clinging to the erroneous idea of a distant male god, Westerners are beginning to realize through self-knowledge and self-actualization that the human form that God takes is each one of us. We are that. There is no separation except for the separation we create within our minds by banishing God to some distant "heaven." Now that we can predict and somewhat contain natural disasters, God no longer seems so terrifying and we can experience the divine presence—and ourselves and each other—as love.

Divine Cooperation

If each of us is one of the elements of supreme beingness, then cooperation is the key that will open our next stage of evolution. If we could see ourselves and each other as ideas in the mind of God, we would know from personal experience of our own thought processes, that ideas interact with one another in a lively field of energy, which could be called feeling or emotion attached to specific ideas.

One could draw an analogy this way: a thinking creator manipulates the mental elements and attempts to form a new pattern. As we have sometimes seen in cooperative efforts between individuals, manipulation rarely works well and leads to confusion and frustration within the group. Some give up; some believe there really is no problem to be solved; others consider a weak solution acceptable; and still others turn their attention elsewhere to gather more data to bring to bear on issues at hand. More creative solutions are facilitated by moving the mind's focus away from the problem and letting acknowledged ideas "incubate" in the creative energy field of the unconscious. In this way, friction is overcome and ideas can flow freely without external manipulations being imposed on them.

If one can experience being an individual idea in the mind of god and maintain an image of oneself as having access to all knowledge, logic can be abandoned occasionally and intuition can be allowed to operate. When we come to a point of harmony or illumination in this state, we experience a cognition that carries emotional conviction of its correctness—in other words, it feels good.

An important thing to remember is that as the individual ideas that take form as human beings attempt to cooperate with one another to co-create our reality, we may feel confusion, frustration, impatience, anger, pain, fatigue, or even exhaustion and despair. There is always tension as friction is overcome. It is a natural part of the creative process. At these times, it is essential that we not feel inadequate and give up.

Creativity is a basic factor in the human makeup—educators assume that everyone has the potential to be in touch with the universal creative field and to act creatively. It could benefit society to establish learning situations that facilitate this creative openness, whether it be the stimulation of ideas within the individual mind, or our cooperation as ideas in an omniscient mind—the "collective consciousness," as Carl Jung called it.

By the same token, religion offers its believers a special union of the physical world with the spiritual. But one goal in our evolutionary image may be that we will need no special union with the spiritual world because it will be our natural experience. We cannot be separate. We don't have to "believe" in flowers because we can see them with our own eyes. Now is the time for us to experience ourselves as spiritual beings in this same way. Westerners have evolved from group-oriented people to human beings who attach so much importance to our own personalities that it causes us to feel isolated and alienated from each other. This idea of separation permeates every aspect of our lives.

Our bodies seem to separate our minds from each other. However, mind is not so much a thing as it is a function. It does not occupy space; neither is it visible or tangible. Mind might be considered akin to potential, for here we find curiosity, purpose, conscience, creativity, reason, intelligence, and perceptual and conceptual thinking. Physicist C. S. Sherrington wrote, "Why should mind have a body? The answer may well run: to mediate between it and other minds."

Chapter 2
End Notes

[1]R. M. Bucke, *Cosmic Consciousness*. Secaucus, N.J.: Citadel Press, 1973.

[2]R. D. Laing, "The Lies of Love," *East West—The Journal of Natural Health and Living*, August, 1987, p. 36.

[3]H. J. Irwin, "ESP and the Human Information Processing System," *Journal of the American Society for Psychical Research*, 1978, 72, pp. 111–126; and "Psi, Attention, and Processing Capacity," *Journal of the American Society for Psychical Research*, 1978, 72, pp. 301–313.

[4]J. S. Bruner, R. R. Oliver, & P. M. Greenfield, *Studies in Cognitive Growth*. New York: Wiley, 1966.

[5]W. W. Keele, "Movement Control in Skilled Motor Performance," *Psychological Bulletin*, 1968, 70, pp. 387–403.

[6]Jack A. Adams, *Human Memory*. New York: McGraw-Hill, 1967, pp. 218–219.

[7]J. P. Guilford, *Personality*. New York: McGraw-Hill, 1959, p. 368.

[8]S. D. Kahn, "'Myers' Problem' Revisited," in *Parapsychology: Its Relationship to Physics, Biology, Psychology, and Psychiatry*, ed. G. R. Schmeidler. Metuchen, N.J.: Scarecrow Press, 1976.

[9]Frederick C. Bartlett, "The Measurement of Human Skill," *British Medical Journal*, June 21, 1947, p. 877.

[10]U. T. Place, "The Concept of Heed," *British Journal of Psychology*, 45, 1954, p. 247.

[11]Michael I. Posner, *Cognition: An Introduction*. Glenview, IL: Scott, Foresman & Co., 1973, pp. 24–25.

[12]Stefan Figar, "The Application of Plethysmography to the Objective Study of So-called Extrasensory Perception," *Journal of the Society for Psychical Research*, 40, 1959, pp. 162–174.

[13]E. D. Dean, "The Plethysmography as an Indicator of ESP," *Journal of the Society for Psychical Research*, 41, 1962, pp. 351–352; "Plethysmography Recordings as ESP Responses," *International Journal of Neuropsychiatry*, 2, 1966, pp. 439–447; and "Plethysmography Results over 3,000 Miles," *Journal of Parapsychology*, 31, 1967.

[14]E. D. Dean and C. B. Nash, "Coincident Plethysmography Results under Controlled Conditions," *Journal of the Society for Psychical Research*, 44, 1967, pp. 1–13.

[15]John Roddam, *The Changing Mind*. Boston: Little, Brown, 1966, pp. 189–190.

[16]Ingo Swann, *Natural ESP*. New York: Bantam Books, 1987.

[17]Roddam, *op. cit.*, p. 195.

Chapter III

RECOGNIZE YOUR POTENTIAL

It has been suggested that we are using only one percent of our human potential. There is little information on why this is so or how we can use more of our potential. It has been ascertained that a brain can only realize its potential if it has a particular kind of body with the following qualities: sensitivity, warm-bloodedness, hands with opposable thumbs, and stereoscopic vision. Thus, human beings have all the basic parts required for realizing their potential.

ESP and Spiritualitity

Our individual minds seem to be conscious and somewhat intelligent, but it is possible that there is a source of intelligence in this universe that exists as pure consciousness. Our minds may only reflect that source. If this were true, all knowledge would be objective. If we allow the source to reflect through us as direct knowing, it does not mean that we are being subjective about our experiences.

In view of the possibility of a single source of universal intelligence that exists as pure consciousness, one can begin to postulate all kinds of psychological applications. For example, one psychological goal might be to help people calm racing thoughts or obsessive thinking by letting that source of pure consciousness lead us to right actions and right relationships.

How might we tap into the resource of universal intelligence or pure consciousness?

There is increasing interest in ESP abilities. Many classes are now available on how to develop ESP abilities and how we might use them for practical purposes. However, many spiritual authorities regard the desire for or attainment of ESP abilities or psychic powers as an obstacle to spiritual growth. Such abilities are sometimes considered to be pure ego gratification and therefore not conducive to a selfless, dedicated life. However, if we could consider the attainment of "direct knowing abilities" to be as natural as the attainment of sensory abilities, we might be able to transcend this idea that one kind of ability is an aid to better living and another is a detriment. Let's think of ESP as an extended human ability, no less natural to us than walking. Neither ability is more important or dangerous than the other.

Sometimes people use drugs to gain insight into psychic and spiritual realms. While many may catch a glimpse of another reality under the influence of drugs, there is a real nonphysical as well as a physical danger in approaching spirituality in this manner. When you are not able to recreate such psychic or spiritual experience on your own, you may not only begin to doubt its reality and become confused, you may continue to drug yourself hoping to recapture your experience until you are totally deluded and out of touch with any agreed-on reality. You may become depressed and isolated, and such an experiment could leave you spiritless, heartless, and apathetic to life.

The Pervasiveness of ESP

Before we can develop any extended human ability, we have to first recognize it. For the purposes of this chapter, I would like to define ESP abilities as "unrecognized human potential." ESP abilities appear to be inherent in all human beings. We may have trouble recognizing them not because they occur so infrequently but rather because they are so all pervasive. To *re*-cognize is to perceive clearly that which was previously known. I often say that it is not the experience of ESP that is lacking—but rather the realization and accurate interpretation of it.

Dr. Louisa Rhine, whose husband was noted parapsychologist J. B. Rhine, wrote an excellent book, entitled *The Invisible Picture*,[1] in which she helps us to understand and interpret our ESP experiences. One important point she makes is that it is the product and not the process of ESP of which we are aware. You may not understand how you are doing it, but once you can verify your impressions, you know it was done. In this respect, ESP resembles normal sense perception and memory. How do you recall a name? You don't know the process, but when the name appears in consciousness you instantly recognize it. What we want to do is learn to stop invalidating ESP and to recognize it even if we don't know exactly how it occurs.

For instance, we trained ourselves for years and years to move our bodies in a precisely coordinated manner—walking, running, sleeping, eating, etc. In fact, we do not know exactly how we do it. We know that when we decide to move our bodies, we can move any way we choose, but the individual incremental movements in this physical process are totally beyond our comprehension. One of the scientifically established ESP abilities is psychokinesis, the ability of the mind to manipulate matter. Is it not possible that movement of the human body is a psychokinetic effect?

We take it for granted we know how to use our bodies and in many cases we believe we are our bodies. I challenge this widely held assumption by virtue of the fact that it took years to learn how to move our bodies with any precision. Physical movements may be potentially natural, but they had to be practiced and practiced to become controlled abilities.

As infants, we moved our eyes first and then our heads. Then we learned to use our arms and legs, fingers and toes. We could sit up first, then crawl, then stand, then walk, but it took months and months of constant effort. We were all little scientists studying the properties of matter, first seeing it, touching it, tasting it, trying to understand what we had to deal with on this planet. Sometimes we became frustrated because we couldn't learn as fast as we wanted to and often burst into unrestrained crying. Thank goodness when we arrived on this planet a support team was provided to help us through this difficult adjustment stage.

When we tried to walk and fell down, no one said, "See, I told you, you couldn't do it." No one even suggested that it was impossible to learn to walk even though it took daily practice over months. We were encouraged in every way to develop our physical abilities and were given directions by those who had already mastered their own. Of course, their motivation was to have us be less dependent on them.

Try to remember the joy of discovering a new ability. Try to reexperience how you learned sensory skills—how persistent you were, how determined you were, the curiosity that demanded your dedication to daily practice, how everything was learned on a gradient from the most simple movement to the most complex.

Learning to talk is just one of the "seemingly miraculous" abilities we have. I read in *The Speech Chain* "...the primary biological function of the vocal organs is not speech production. They developed first to perform other vital services, such as breathing, chewing, and swallowing. Only later were they applied to the production of speech."[2] We learned to use our larynx to break the steady air stream from our lungs into a series of puffs, which produced the audible sound which we use in speech. If this doesn't sound like learning to do the impossible, I don't know what does.

If we had similar support networks and encouraging environments in which to recognize and develop our extrasensory abilities, it is possible we could learn to use these as effectively as we have learned to use our "sensory" skills. Why are we content to stop learning at the sensory level?

It could be that we don't have any reason to develop the scientifically established ESP abilities of telepathy, clairvoyance, precognition, or psychokinesis. But surely such abilities could be very useful.

The Fear of ESP

There seems to be an ethics problem blocking us here. Three-quarters of the U.S. population confess belief in ESP, but there is still a prevalent fear of it. Fear is a common response to the discovery of powerful energies.

Are we afraid that ESP will mean we can move about as invisible beings, free from the restrictions of our bodies, invading privacy or doing destructive things? Until we address the ethical problems posed by ESP phenomena, we will continue to be afraid of them, and thus the media will continue to portray such experiences in negative, destructive ways, continuing the fear chain.

We are projecting our own fears about ESP phenomena, rather than considering possible constructive uses for such abilities. It is essential that we discuss the reasons for our fear of ESP abilities if we are ever to learn how to release them for creative and productive purposes.

Neighborhood support groups formed by those with an understanding of invisible, creative abilities may sound revolutionary, but so did women's support groups in the sixties, and so did AIDS support groups five years ago. They are no longer considered revolutionary. However, as long as we continue to shy away from discussing our fears and learning how to use our abilities in positive, nonthreatening ways, we are going to be limited.

The media could, of course, greatly facilitate an evolutionary breakthrough for humanity if it would address the issues with the serious, in-depth coverage presently allocated to issues of war and destruction. However, since there is no widespread support from the media at this time, we need to study our own human experiences by ourselves and in groups and break through the barriers erected to separate us from our "extended human abilities."

Most of us have hunches or uncanny experiences, which we generally discard or invalidate because they are not logical. Most human beings are already using intuitive thinking, but such thinking has been largely discredited in the past by male scientists who valued only logic. This is an important observation, because women are physiologically more capable of translating intuitive thought into language than men and this could be one reason why men so often say they cannot understand the way women think. It also explains why women are commonly judged to be more adept at using their intuitive resources. Men and women actually do think differently.

Many of us probably make decisions based on intuitive perceptions without realizing it. This is one type of potential that has been brought to actualization and yet is only now emerging from blatant malignment and derisive invalidation.

If you can tolerate ambiguity or approach fear of the unknown with courage, and if you want to develop your personal extended human abilities, first find out everything you possibly can about the way you operate. Are you a visual or an auditory type? Do you remember well? Do you remember more easily what you see or only what you hear? Is it easier to remember if you do something muscular, like writing the information down? How do you think and what do you think about most of the time?

How Does Your Mind Work?

There are three main ways of "knowing." TRY THIS LITTLE EXPERIMENT. *What is a very large four-legged animal that supposedly never forgets?* Now, try to realize how that information came to you.

If you are an *auditory* or *verbal* type, you may have heard the word "elephant" as if uttered internally. If you are a *visual* type, you may have seen the printed word "elephant" in your mind or formed a mental picture of an elephant.

If you usually receive information by a *motor* encoding system, you might have imagined touching an elephant or have felt the movements of your own larynx uttering the word "elephant."

Let's try one more: If I suggest the word "danger" to you, how is that developed in your mind? Stop reading for a moment and watch what your mind does with the word "danger."

Did you hear voices or alarming sounds? Did you

see violent people or animals advancing? Maybe you felt chills or gooseflesh. There are other forms of knowing in a sensory way, such as smelling fire when I say the word "danger." Your response to the word or idea would be based to a large extent on your past experience, as well as your particular cognitive style. For instance, some people learn from reading, some have to have things explained to them, and some must be shown and actually have some kind of hands-on experience before they can grasp a concept. Basically we all code and store cognitive information verbally, visually, and with muscle movements. Although we may prefer one mode over another, we probably use all three methods in combination.

Visual and verbal memory codes are easy to understand, but motor memory codes are a little different since they are unconscious. When you learned to ride a bike, watching people riding didn't help, hearing them tell you how they rode didn't help—the only way you mastered the skill was to get up there and learn to balance your body on a moving bike. You learn this kind of ability through your muscles or motor system and once you encode this skill, you don't forget it as easily as you might forget information acquired visually or verbally. The ability to type or play a musical instrument is also learned through motor coordination, so you can do it without thinking about it and you don't forget how to do it either.

Sometimes when we get ESP information, it comes in the form of a picture in front of our eyes or behind our eyes, as a sort of hallucination or mental image. Sometimes we hear words warning us or giving us needed information. These can also be heard as if they came from outside or inside our bodies. And sometimes, we simply find ourselves moving to a location without any conscious reasoning, only to discover when we arrive that we are needed or that there is someone or something there that we needed. "Need" is the important word here. Need is a basic concept throughout nature and needs tend to fulfill themselves, sometimes via ESP.

Information can be obtained consciously or unconsciously in these three different ways. Examples of *unconscious knowing* can be seen from information derived in dreams or in the carrying out of posthypnotic suggestions. In the latter case, people are unaware of what they are doing. The suggestion is externalized in automatic movements which the conscious person can neither control, understand, or explain. ESP abilities are also often performed spontaneously without comprehension and without being able to control or explain them.

In posthypnotic suggestion, we can inspire either a motor action (take off your shoe) or a sensory hallucination (see or hear something that isn't there). Hallucination has no negative connotation here; it is merely defined as "sensory experience with no known physical basis." Similarly, an extrasensory perception may be defined as the obtaining of information that is not accessible by means of any known sense.

To continue with your self-exploration, you may ask other specific questions about how you operate. For instance, when you dance, do you move freely to the beat of the music or do you do dance-step patterns you have learned? How spontaneous are you in other ways? What is your main point of interest? What is it that excites you more than anything else?

Once you discover your point of interest, operate more and more from that base. Awareness of your memory patterns and retrieving your childhood spontaneity will enable you to recognize and develop your intuitive abilities. When you know how you process information in general, you will be better able to deal with ESP and intuitive communications.

ESP in Everyday Life

Here are some practical ways to start using your extrasensory abilities in your daily life.

TRY A FEW OF THESE EXPERIMENTS.

Experiment 1. We all misplace items occasionally. If you lose your keys, after you look in all the possible places where they might be and they aren't there, don't panic—concentrate on the keys and ask your intuitive self where they are. Then do something else; divert your conscious attention. Expect the answer to come to mind or that your body will be directed to the keys. This usually works quite well, and you won't have to work yourself up into a state of anxiety looking furiously for something that has been mislaid. Your hand may know where it put the object, even though your head doesn't.

This process is called "incubation." Albert Einstein used a similar technique in seeking answers to theoretical problems—and maybe when looking for his keys. First, you announce your problem to your subliminal self (Where are my keys?). Then wait quietly and watch and listen—OR go and do something else, but be alert and expect the answer to come at any minute. Remember your hand knows where you put the keys down, but your mind doesn't have the picture yet.

The Importance of Dreams

Even if you find it difficult, if not impossible, to remember your dreams, we all dream every night. You can find out a lot about yourself and significant others by learning to remember your dreams. A positive correlation has been found between how well a person can recall dreams and ESP success in a laboratory.

Precognitive dreaming is the most commonly reported ESP experience in our society. A precognitive dream is one in which you get information about a future event that is later verified. In other words, at present, we are most comfortable with an unconscious ESP ability displaced into the future.

Experiment 2. Tell yourself before you go to sleep that you are going to remember and write down your dreams. Keep a pen and paper easily accessible beside your bed, and try not to move too quickly when you awaken. By writing down a dream, or even part of a dream, as soon as you wake up, you will begin to remember details that could easily be forgotten later.

You may be receiving information in your dreams that your conscious mind cannot accept. If you choose to gain information this way, you may have to overcome resistance to writing down dreams immediately upon awakening—sometimes in the middle of the night. Just keep telling yourself gently that this is a good way to learn more about who you are.

If you can't recall your dreams at first, you might set an alarm clock for three A.M. some night when you don't have to get up in the morning, or try to sleep an hour or so longer than usual. This often enhances dream recall. With consistent effort, you will be able to recall more and more of your dreams. Keep them in a journal or looseleaf notebook if you like, and date them. Reread them from time to time and pay close attention to recurrent themes, images, and symbols. Dialogue with key dream elements with pencil and paper, writing down whatever comes to mind. Let your own dream symbols tell you what they mean and how they relate to events and feelings in your life and to those close to you. Knowledge of dreams can also help you make decisions by showing you what your intuitive thoughts and feelings are.

Extrasensory experiences happen to all of us, but we tend to invalidate them rather than recognize and record them to check on their mode and frequency. For instance, how many times have you known who it was before you answered the phone, or been about to call someone who called you right then? Perhaps you've had letters crossing in the mail between you and someone at a distance whom you care about. Some people call these events coincidences and leave it at that. To "coincide" is to occupy the same place in space or time, to correspond in nature, or to be in accord or agreement. We are all probably more connected than we realize.

Modern physicists and psychologists have shown that mind-to-mind and mind-over-matter communications, as well as mind transcending time and space, are real possibilities. Don't sabotage your potential intuitive power by making such experiences seem ridiculous, casting them aside as frivolous, or downright disbelieving evidence of their reality when it is presented to you. Be skeptical by all means, but break through the barrier of denial.

The Value of Skepticism

There are two forms of skepticism. A benevolent skeptic will take the time to explore a concept before forming opinions about it. A destructive skeptic will dismiss evidence prior to investigation. Astrophysicist Carl Sagan, one of America's leading skeptics regarding paranormal phenomena, stated in 1987:

> If you are only skeptical, then no new ideas make it through to you. You never learn anything new. You become a crotchety old person convinced that nonsense is ruling the world. (There is, of course, much data to support you.) But every now and then, maybe once in a hundred cases, a new idea turns out to be on the mark, valid and wonderful. If you are too much in the habit of being skepti-

cal about everything, you are going to miss or resent it, and either way you will be standing in the way of understanding and progress. On the other hand, if you are open to the point of gullibility and have not an ounce of skeptical sense in you, then you cannot distinguish the useful ideas from the worthless ones. If all ideas have validity then you are lost, because then, it seems to me, no ideas have any validity at all.[3]

Sagan belongs to the Committee for the Scientific Investigation of Claims of the Paranormal (CSICOP, pronounced *psi cop*). This group has appointed itself as official police, authorized to disclaim ESP. I have yet to learn of much scientific investigation into ESP by the members of this committee.

We need to personally investigate our extended human abilities. Each one of us must do it for ourselves. We cannot rely on psychics or traditional scientists to do it for us. Conscious evolutionary thinking demands that as we learn, each one of us is responsible for assisting at least one other person on the path of self-awareness.

Detecting Potential

1. **Pay attention to "out of the blue" thoughts that pop into your head.** If the idea of the hula hoop had come to you, would you have aborted the idea as foolish or made millions of dollars? The first step is noticing what appear to be strange ideas.

2. **The ideas will have to be different enough from your everyday life to stand out.** For instance, if you dream about a blonde friend as a brunette and the next time you see her she has tinted her hair, it's probably not intuition if she is in the habit of chang-

ing her hair color. It probably is intuition if she has never changed her hair color before.

3. **Use visualization techniques to bring into your life objects or events you desire.** Concentrate on the event happening, see it clearly in your mind's eye, let it go, and get on with your life in quiet expectation. Repeat daily.

4. **Verify your experiences.** Get them out of your head and into the physical world and you will avoid a lot of confusion as to whether or not they really happened. Write experiences down and date them, or tell somebody what you dreamed and that it may possibly be precognitive. Having outside witnesses or documentation helps you to increase your conviction in your abilities. However, do not tell people who will automatically put you down. To choose to do this is evidence of your own resistance and self-sabotage.

5. **A sympathetic group is a good place to gain support in your efforts to develop more powerful modes of thinking.** If someone in your group is blocking personal intuition (or insecure in trusting it), other group members might share how they overcame those same barriers and unique. Being in a group will also prevent you from feeling alone. One of the main fears about delving into other concepts of reality is the sense of being isolated from one's peers. This fear could cause you to eliminate intuitive thoughts and decrease your mental power. We all like to feel comfortable, which is why connecting with a like-minded group can be so valuable.

Here are a few more examples of experiments you can try in order to check out your abilities.

Experiment 3. When the phone rings, without thinking, verbalize the first name that comes to your mind. Keep a little score pad by the phone and mark down whether you are right.

Experiment 4. When you're waiting at a bank of

elevators, try to guess which will come first. Keep track of how many times you are right.

At this point, it's not really necessary to mark down your wrong responses unless you want to, but you might want to note factors that are conducive to the accuracy of your extended human abilities. Training extrasensory abilities could be like training a child to walk. When a child falls down, you don't tell her she did it wrong; you encourage her to try again, saying something like, "You almost made it that time." Through adequate encouragement, plenty of practice, and no lack of faith, she will certainly walk at some point. So, be happy and accept the child's growing ability, knowing that it will get increasingly better and be useful to her for the rest of her life. She'll soon be running and may even one day break track records. Or maybe she'll be dancing and become the world's greatest ballerina. So, as you learn ESP abilities, don't be harsh and critical of yourself. Treat yourself like a small child learning to walk for the first time. Practice diligently, knowing that you will accomplish what you've set out to do, and wait faithfully and expectantly for success.

Experiment 5. The next time you are waiting for a bus or a ride, you can stretch out your visual and sensory perceptions as far as they will go in the direction of the unseen vehicle. Try to locate the bus on its route. Stretching your sensory perceptions may strengthen your psychic awareness. It's not so different from exercising a muscle and finding new strength and power in that muscle.

You can take an active or passive role with your ESP abilities. If you are trying to decide whether or not to act on mental impressions that may be ESP messages, bear this in mind. It has been determined that the less information there is in the message, the more conviction there is in the action.

You have more conviction when you are acting on

an emotion or compulsion rather than visual or verbal information. A message may come with complete detail of time, place, person, and action; or register as emotional or physical upset for no known reason; or surface as a compulsion to act in a certain way without knowing why; or create a physical effect in the room with no reasonable explanation. This last effect might be like a clock stopping at the exact time of death of a distant relative. These are the main ways ESP messages will present themselves to you.

The important thing to remember is that one person may experience ESP in a visual mode, another in a verbal mode, a third person may have an intuition, while a fourth may simply feel upset and act on that uneasiness. Do not try to pattern your ESP experiences after anyone else's. Learn your own ESP style. It's like finding your own personal gold mine.

A useful analogy might be the difference between going to school and learning a trade or getting involved with people who do this kind of work and assisting them until you learn the trade. Both ways are correct, but one will feel more right for you. The same principles apply to ESP; by being yourself and tuning into your own unique ESP abilities you can claim a new level of self-actualization.

Direct Knowing

Off the dance floor and back in the office... parapsychologist Rex Stanford has proposed a theory of ESP that he calls "psi-mediated instrumental response" (PMIR) theory. It states that people "nonintentionally use ESP to scan the environment for need-relevant objects or events or for information crucially related to such events, and that when such information is obtained, they act in ways which are instrumental in satisfying their needs. They do this without conscious effort to use ESP, without conscious effort to fulfill the need, without conscious awareness of the need or of the need-relevant circumstances, and without realizing that anything extraordinary is happening."[4]

Other people call it an unconscious or "direct knowing" ability, and it is usually accomplished in the most efficient and economical way possible. It gets you to the right place at the right time to be with the right people to do the right thing. I have met people in this manner who turned out to be quite important in my life. In order to do this, I had to free up a sense of timing that told me I should be doing something else at that moment. I had to be willing to make a mistake, take a wrong turn, become anxious that I was lost or wasting time. I had to be willing to know that I don't know everything consciously. Wonderful meetings can take place under these circumstances. And unavailable, but needed information can be obtained that one could have no conscious idea of how to get.

Direct knowing ability can manifest itself in several different ways. One might be that your timing is thrown off so that you arrive unexpectedly at an appropriate place to encounter a favorable event or to avoid an unfavorable one.

You might forget or remember to do something. For instance, you may have reminded yourself for weeks to check the air in your tires. One day you actually do it, even though you're in a hurry as usual. You stop at a gas station long enough to do this and thereby avoid being on a bridge up ahead where a fallen cable has caused accidents and a traffic tie-up. This not only involves remembering to do something, but your timing has also been affected.

You might make a mistake and make room for the ability to operate. For instance, I read of a case in which a teenager misdialed in telephoning a friend and reached an elderly woman who was having a heart attack. The woman was barely able to get to the phone, but did so, crying out for help and collapsing on the floor. The teenager had the operator trace the call and thus was able to send help. The woman's life was saved.

You might be trying to solve a problem and, to rest for a while from the dilemma, you may decide to call a friend to chat. In this conversation, you may learn some unanticipated news of special importance to you and it may even have a direct bearing on your problem.

Or you may get an idea or image, or a feeling that is so unusual or inappropriate to your life that you may give it more meaning. A dream might be extra vivid and turn out to be precognitive.

This unconscious knowing ability will probably not work as well for you if you are too rigid or inhibited, or behave in a ritualistic or stereotypical fashion. Also, certain factors dispose one toward systematic misuse of the ability in ways that would normally be regarded as against one's own best interests. Some examples would be self-destructive tendencies, a negative self-image, withheld emotions such as guilt, fear, or anger, or an approach-avoidance conflict. Whether you approach or avoid the object or event that will fulfill your need probably depends on the same factors that govern your behavior in ordinary approach-avoidance situations. Do you approach your goal enthusiastically or keep backing off in everyday life? For example, a child sees a dog and runs toward it smiling. As he gets nearer he becomes afraid and slows down, and ultimately stops and then moves away, apparently out of fear of being bitten. People are often more motivated to avoid unfamiliar situations than to approach them.

The PMIR theory suggests that ESP phenomena may not be paranormal, rare, or bizarre, but much more frequent and integral in the scheme of the things than we have imagined. ESP may be like the air we breathe. We can't see it; we don't think about it much; but it is vital to every second of our lives.

Persistence Is the Key to Progress

It is going to take time, effort, and courage to realize your individual ESP potential. You may face some loneliness and isolation as a pioneer in conscious evolution. There is a certain risk involved in not conforming to others' ideas about who you are. You may experience feelings of anxiety and self-doubt that will rock you. Hold on! Nothing ventured; nothing gained. Stand firm in your convictions concerning your potential. Don't let others dissuade you from your chosen inquiry into life. When enough of us reach a point of understanding about our essential beingness, we will not be so alone. It's comparable to the tale of the hundredth monkey—at some point, consciousness will shift and things we hold true today may be irrelevant in our new concept of reality. We will derive strength when the power of this new reality claims us.

Our self-image may be transformed from inadequacy and limitation to one of communication with and access to everything that is. With a more thorough investigation of the uncharted realms of human experience—individually and collectively, subjectively and objectively—we could enhance our experience of unity with one another and truly liberate ourselves to express the natural infinite potential and purpose we were created to express.

Chapter 3
End Notes

[1]L. E. Rhine, *The Invisible Picture*. Jefferson, NC: McFarland, 1981.

[2]Peter B. Denes and E. N. Pinson, *The Speech Chain*. New York: Anchor Books, 1973, p. 54.

[3]Carl Sagan, in his keynote address at the 1987 annual conference of the committee for the Scientific Investigation of Claims of the Paranormal.

[4]Rex B. Stanford, "An Experimentally Testable Model for Spontaneous Psi Events. I. Extrasensory Events," *Journal of the American Society for Physical Research*, 68, 1974, pp. 34–57.

Chapter IV

EXPRESS YOUR ABILITIES

How can we use our ESP abilities to improve the quality of our daily lives? It may be centuries before we understand the exact processes of ESP, but it is now possible to find constructive means of employing our abilities. Ironically, Russian scientists seem much more amenable to researching practical applications of ESP abilities than parapsychologists here in the U.S. The fundamental process of how electricity really works is unknown to this day, but nevertheless it has changed the life of everyone who has access to it, and knows where the switch is and which way to flip it for "on." I believe that people are constantly using ESP without knowing its process. Most seem to be using what Rex Stanford calls PMIR, or direct knowing ability.

At present in the U.S., ESP abilities are being used for locating natural resources. Geologists and seismologists found in the 1970s that 48 percent of all oil wells paid for themselves and 49 percent were dry holes, while only 3 percent were profit producing—and they went prospecting for novel exploration techniques. ESP specialists have discovered oil, gas, and mineral deposits by ascertaining what is beneath the earth through extended sensory means. Although it is not unusual to call in a dowser to find water, using similar clairvoyant abilities to discover more profitable resources is often questioned. However, ESP resource exploration continues with little or no publicity.

In police stations across the country, people with ESP capacities are cooperating in criminal investigations. In stranger-to-stranger murder cases where no clues are available, police often use ESP specialists to get any leads they possibly can. ESP is also used for making medical diagnoses and healing; for aiding executives in decision making and stock market predictions; and even for space exploration.

The most common individual uses of ESP are: gaining information about loved ones, especially in crisis situations; for our own survival and protection, as indicated in studies of precognition and avoidance of railway accidents; and for the betterment and enrichment of our lives through mental visualization. Well-known ESP specialist and author Harold Sherman was the foremost advocate of our learning how to turn our dreams into realities by picturing our heartfelt desires in our minds, and then allowing these images to recreate reality—a sort of psychokinetic effect on life. He practiced these principles successfully and the results were evident throughout his life.[1]

Attitudes and ESP

There are specific attitudes that can facilitate the expression of one's abilities once they have been recognized. Researchers have found that people who are cheerful, sociable, adventurous, enthusiastic, confident, alert, responsive, and easygoing are able to expand their concept of reality with less effort than those with the opposite characteristics. If you want

ESP to work for you, try to steer clear of rigid and inhibited ways of thinking, feeling and behaving. Those who talk, act, and think positively may be using their abilities to put themselves in the right place at the right time, making sound decisions to enrich their lives. This could be why some people have better "luck" than others.

The famous psychologist, H. J. Eysenck, discovered that extroverts score higher on ESP than introverts. If one is open to impressions with a free, uncritical readiness to respond, one can also expect better results. Those who are withdrawn from life in general tend to withdraw from ESP targets as well, and they score poorly.

ESP is also affected by moods, attitudes, and beliefs. One of the few things known about ESP is that people who believe in ESP score higher than those who don't believe it can happen.

If testing conditions are congenial, ESP scores are generally higher. Emotional closeness seems to be an important but not a necessary prerequisite for ESP. If you like the person you are working with, ESP scores will be higher—but they will always depend on your expectations and those of the experimenter.

Unforced, spontaneous impressions are more likely to be correct for ESP than impressions obtained by forced, dutiful obedience. A relaxed, accepting attitude seems to facilitate ESP. People with more defense mechanisms in operation tend to get lower ESP scores. If you can recall your dreams, you are probably more open to your mental processing and will probably do better with ESP. You may also have a better facility than most for realizing and remembering your ESP experiences. Also, people score better at an ESP task they like as opposed to one they dislike.

If you are normally a visualizer (have a vivid imagination and see mental images clearly), your ESP will probably operate better through visual imagery. If you are more of an abstract association-type thinker, your ESP impressions will probably come in the form of words. If you are an action-oriented person, you may feel a compulsion to do something rather than to think something, when an ESP impression occurs.

If you are usually composed, you might do better at ESP when you are in a state of arousal. If you are habitually tense and anxious, the ESP setting should be calm and peaceful. Anxious people score better with a neutral target than with an arousing one.

A participant's scoring rate seems to be independent of the degree of complexity of an ESP task. You can't make ESP any more complex or difficult than it already is by nature.

Transcending Societal Stereotypes

The psychological concept of androgyny has been proposed by several researchers to refer to the integration of "masculine" and "feminine" characteristics in a person of either sex. Some theorists have suggested that androgyny may correlate with fully actualized psychological functioning, creativity, maturity, social adjustment, and autonomy. There is some evidence to suggest freedom from stereotyped sex-roles may be intimately linked with the type of psychological freedom necessary for ESP development and expression. It seems that male or female sensitives who can transcend societal concepts of reality by producing verified ESP phenomena in laboratories can also transcend societal sex-role stereotypical thinking and behavior as measured by S. L. Bem's "Androgyny Scale."[2]

Another factor in ESP receptivity is relaxation. Progressive relaxation and reduced sensory stimuli techniques such as those used in a Ganzfeld procedure have been shown to be conducive to successful ESP demonstrations. When your body is relaxed and your mind is alert to internal thinking processes, you will probably be better able to gain access to other than logical information.

Experiments in ESP Receptivity

If you're going to set up home experiments, find yourself a quiet place with very little external sensory input. Do a little deep breathing, then alternate tensing and relaxing all your muscles sequentially, from your toes to your forehead. This should help put you in a receptive state.

1. You might want to ask a friend to place an object or picture that you have not seen in his or her home in a specified place and then wonder about what that might be every once in a while for a day or so, trying to pick up the correct image. When you least expect it, you may see the object in your mind. Specific details of the experiment should be decided on by the two parties before the actual test. Simple objects and pictures should be used. We might suggest simple designs made from different colors of construction paper on a contrasting background for first attempts. You may actually experience yourself as going to your friend's home and viewing the target—don't be surprised. You could get the target information by telepathy, clairvoyance, or exterior vision as in an out-of-body experience, but expect it with confidence and watch attentively for it.

Ingo Swann, one of America's most talented ESP specialists, claims that a pet chinchilla caused him to decide ESP was possible and he was determined to find out all about it. This story is related in his book *To Kiss Earth Goodbye*.

2. If you have a pet, you might experiment with directing mental messages to it. For instance, you

might try to get it to go from one room to another by your silent desire that it do so. When it is at a visible distance, mentally tell it to sit down or perform some other action. Be careful not to give the animal any sensory cues by physical movement or sound. Sit or stand very quietly, relax, and think about establishing some telepathic rapport with your pet.

3. Maybe you have plants around your house or work space and if so, work on them mentally. See that the plants you are working with receive the same amount of sunlight, food, and water as other plants. It would be best if you could start from seeds, but two plants of the same type and size will be O.K. for your first try. Talk to one of them, touch it, and encourage it to grow in good health. See if it prospers better than the emotionally neglected plant because of your positive PK influence.

4. If these experiments work, you may want to try encouraging the health and growth of people you know. On a regular basis, send positive, healing energy to someone who is sick, having an operation, or in a depressed state of mind. Visualize that person as spiritually whole and sound. Try sending this positive energy at a time when the other person might be more receptive, such as when the person expresses a desire for good health.

Some people prefer illness to health; bondage to freedom. There are many reasons for this. Those who are ill may not know any other way to get attention or to exercise power and control over their environments. Freedom demands personal responsibility. Help the person break through to a desire for healthy, purposeful living. Whether you are actually sending healing PK energy or activating the person's capacity for self-healing by sending positive telepathic messages, know that a healing principle is present in each of us. If we know the principle, we can apply it in daily life.

In the New Testament we read of many who were

sent forth to cure diseases and cast out demons. This is not merely the work of priests, ministers, and physicians. We can minister to ourselves and to one another, if we will. Some people claim that touching the ill person works better, as in charismatic healing, but this does not appear to be absolutely necessary. Holding a healthy image of the person in your mind may be equally effective.

5. Perhaps you would like to use your abilities to win the lottery, or at the track or casino. It's O.K. to want to win as long as no harm is done to others. Handling the success of winning will be a new level of responsibility for you. But to learn to win by using mind over matter requires persistent practice.

Most of our evidence for proof of psychokinesis comes from dice experiments. You could start there. Get some dice and put one of them in a dice cup. Shake the cup and try to bounce the die off a backstop of some sort for better random motion. Try to influence a certain number to turn up. Change the number systematically so you are not always trying for the same number. There is a parapsychological controversy as to whether an event such as changing a die face or manipulating lottery numbers is PK or precognition. You could influence the objects directly or know the outcome in advance by future vision. In either case, keep a record of how many times you are right. If you can perfect this ability, the casinos are in a lot of trouble. Visit them irregularly, incognito, and take only winnings that will not attract a lot of attention. After all, you have the rest of your life to win, once you have the ability perfected.

6. Noted Israeli psychic Uri Geller seems to be able to hold broken watches in his hands and make them work again. He also bends spoons, but there is not much call for that in daily life.

Maybe you would like to test out your ability for fixing broken equipment. We all know people who break equipment consistently—a trait labeled "PK-missing"—so why not try for PK-fixing? You could do this with your car, washer, TV, whatever. We would all like to have fewer repair bills. Concentrate on the broken item, touch it if you like, see it working perfectly in your mind's eye, then relax and expect it to happen. Your own method will become clear to you as you work with this possibility.

7. If you want to try to move something without touching it, you should know that it is easier to change the motion of something that is already moving than it is to move an object at rest. A compass needle might be a good place to start. Check your location to see if your compass is free of magnetic pulls from power sources or rumbling vibrations that might move the needle naturally. Set your compass on a stable surface and concentrate on it from a distance. You may turn out to be a power source yourself.

8. For thousands of years, objects have been used for divination purposes. Dowsing rods are used in many areas of the world today. People hire water dowsers to locate underground streams on their property. It's an accepted fact that some people can do this. We don't hear as much about people who dowse for oil, natural gas, or precious minerals. Maybe when people find these products, they are no longer dowsers, but successful prospectors. When such prospectors receive financial reward from their efforts at understanding their inherent abilities, they also receive social acceptance. If there were more commercial uses for ESP information today, we might be able to lay aside the ethical problems often blocking the expression of our abilities.

Some people use dowsing rods over maps, rather than at an actual location. Dowsing is the purest form of clairvoyance; no words, no pictures—just direct knowing that causes a movement. It could be the dowser's intuition, operating through unconscious muscle action, that makes the rod work.

9. Dowsing rods can also be used to answer personal questions, but most people use pendulums for this purpose. Find your own system for determining answers. For example, if the pendulum swings in a clockwise circle it is indicating yes, while a counterclockwise movement indicates no. If it goes in a horizontal line from left to right, it is saying no—a line from forward to back is yes. Start asking questions.

You will know your intuition is working if the answers to your questions are usually accurate and you have no apparent means of knowing these answers. Watch your patterns of behavior, especially if you begin to think discarnate entities are supplying your answers. Caution is advised. Accepting your intuitive abilities will help you know yourself better and become more aware of others. Getting to know this part of yourself will help you stay healthy, happy, and free more often.

Psychosomatic Medicine

You might want to check your ills and pains for psychosomatic symptoms. Doctors and dentists affirm that we can make ourselves ill with our minds and emotions. For example, three of their journals are *Psychosomatic Medicine, Journal of the American Society of Psychosomatic Dentistry and Medicine*, and *Journal of Psychosomatic Research*. There are numerous books that have been written on our ability to make ourselves sick. But there is no scientific journal affirming that we can make ourselves well with our minds. If a patient presents a doctor with a case of healing, the doctor shrugs it off with some phrase such as "spontaneous remission." It is plain to see what is going on here. In the case of psychosomatic illness, they get more patients; in the case of psychosomatic healing, they get fewer patients. Economic determination dictates public information sources. Some doctors at Harvard Medical School and elsewhere are trying to reverse this trend. Studies in the field of psychoneuroimmunology verify that we can make ourselves well with our minds.

Doctors often use language that make your body seem a mystery to you. Do not be confused. Your body is more of a mystery to one who has never seen it than to one who has been intimately connected with it for many years. Watch and listen to your body; it will tell you what is needed for health and happiness and also how you can stop abusing it.

If you find yourself getting a cold every time you plan to visit a particular relative, examine your motivation and desire to go there. If you learn that enhanced human abilities can produce psychosomatic illnesses, you will see that your thoughts and feelings are having an effect on your body. In other words, mental and emotional energy is being used in a destructive manner. Accept the energy, own it, and try to rechannel it in constructive directions. You may miss a few times and cause your car to break down instead of your body so you won't have to go somewhere you don't want to go. Use these clues to start being honest with yourself. Learn to say No when you mean No.

You might create some destruction or distraction in your home or office such as a bookshelf falling or unconsciously breaking your typewriter in order to get a break from work. Be alert. Any of these could be a sign of growth. It might mean you are no longer breaking down your most precious possession—your body—and now the goal is to get this energy moving in a positive direction. This is where you can begin to channel psychokinetic (PK) power. Extend your ability to influence matter almost as if you were exercising a muscle. Challenge it with slightly larger or more difficult tasks to perform each time. The first step is channeling the intuitive powers you already have; the second is extending them.

Responsibility of Power

As your consciousness expands through using your inner knowing—along with your sensory perceptions and factual information—you will realize a power within you to take control of your body and your life. You will be more at home in the world and less battered about by external conditions and other people. You may be tempted to try to exercise control over others, but you will know the wisdom of refraining, because it would only be playing a manipulative game on a mental level. It could backfire, since others have intuition too, and you could end up with a gigantic power play on your hands. There are better ways to spend your time.

This is where your sense of responsibility is so important. Indeed, you will feel compelled to respond to your newly acquired abilities, but power is best expressed through love and wisdom. Paul's advice to the Philippians in the New Testament was this: "...whatever is true, whatever is honorable, whatever is just, whatever is pure, whatever is lovely, whatever is gracious, if there is any excellence, if there is anything worthy of praise, think about these things." Always strive for the best for yourself and others and you will use your intuitive abilities for constructive purposes and not in harmful ways. Once you have established a sound ethical foundation, you will be less fearful as your mental abilities develop rapidly in new directions.

As you master your expanded intuitive abilities, others will be attracted to you. But watch out—a patio lantern offers light, but also draws bugs. Some people may become parasitic as you increase in power. You will have to be aware of them and keep them at a distance from you. There are those who may try to sap your energy, not realizing that equal power is accessible to all. If fatigue comes on you suddenly, check the people around you. If a certain person is around you every time your energy ebbs, be aware to use special precautions around that individual.

Care about the welfare of others, but don't encourage them in their own personal irresponsibility by trying to make things right for them. You might be able to, but it will not be helpful for the personal growth of the person you are protecting. Better to alert them to their own inner power and demand that they respond to life with their own ability to cope and survive. They will be stronger for it and you won't be engaged in a power game for ego gratification. A unitive experience may be shared by two people, but it will not develop out of one person's trying to control the other's behavior.

Negative Uses of ESP

Of course, in the discovery of any new energy, dangers are apparent. Throughout history, in many cultures, spells have been cast for love, money, or revenge. They have worked through the power of suggestion, through the belief systems involved, or possibly by thoughts sent out to the person for whom the spell was cast. If one can heal, can one also harm? Reports of experiments with Nina Kulagina, a Russian PK specialist, would indicate this possibility. It has been reported that she is able to influence the heart of a frog by slowing it down, speeding it up, or stopping it on mental command. It is reported that she has caused blisters to rise on someone else's skin, as well as her own. She has been observed by Western scientists as being able to move small objects across a table by the power of thought alone, so reports of these additional abilities do not seem too farfetched.

ESP phenomena as a source of causing harm to others may sound frightening. It can be. But you may derive a sense of protection in knowing that your positive thinking will decrease the probability of picking up negative thoughts from others. A solid ethical foundation coupled with the chance of possible retribution should prevent you from sending out negativity.

Using psi abilities for political espionage is a real possibility; it has been done in the past. The U.S. military has been interested in psi abilities since the early fifties when the Army asked J. B. Rhine if he could train war dogs to locate buried land mines. He reported above-chance results with the dogs. Psi research has been funded recently by the U.S. Department of Defense and NASA. The CIA also seems interested.

To a pacifist, implications of this kind of activity seem enormous and ominous, but research must continue in good faith. When Einstein realized the destructive possibilities of atomic power, it probably troubled him greatly, but it did not prevent him from sharing his discoveries. While the threat of a nuclear holocaust has been with us for more than a quarter of a century, the worst outcome has been the victims in Hiroshima. During the same amount of time, many valuable uses for atomic energy have been applied, especially in the world of medicine and saving human lives. As we evolve as psychic beings, we will need to proceed with the investigation of psi abilities with this same kind of good faith and begin to teach use of psi power in an ethical manner.

There are other ethical considerations. For instance, should you tell people about intuitions you have of their impending illness, divorce, or misfortune? You always need to use good judgment. Many people seem easily influenced by suggestions. There are such things as self-fulfilling prophecies. This is the belief that something will happen, coupled with a fear of it happening, which might actually make it happen because a person will orient his or her behavior in that direction. Consequently, it can be helpful to recognize that all these emerging abilities can be thought of as laws or principles of action. They are always in operation whether you know it or not. They can be used to any purpose. The point is to recognize this and to start using these principles for the highest good of the most people.

Another example of this use and misuse of ESP can be seen in business. While precognitive flashes can be used for decision making that leads to financial success, subliminal advertising has been banned because it attempts to use mind-to-mind communication to project messages to sell products. Unfortunately, it has not been entirely eliminated.

The government's use of ESP specialists to gather personal information on others could abridge civil liberties. It is therefore important for groups and individuals to realize that developing intuitive abilities does not automatically mean that a *higher* level of consciousness and ethics has been reached. These abilities have probably been part of the evolutionary process all along. Some scientists choose to think of extrasensory perception as primary perception.

If all this is true, what safeguards are there against the unethical use of ESP abilities? First, not everyone is interested in taking the time and effort to develop these abilities. Most people's need for immediate gratification of efforts would probably mean that more traditional methods of crime or harassment would be used by criminals. Second, many spiritual leaders have pointed out that attachment to results often prevents the development of powers. Motivation must be there, but greed could prevent anything from happening. Third, truly intuitive individuals might not be able to cause pain in others without feeling it themselves.

Some people let life happen to them, taking little responsiblity for their quality of life. Other people make life happen. You can *experience* your life or *express* your life. It's your choice.

Chapter 4
End Notes

[1]Harold Sherman, *How to Take Yourself Apart and Put Yourself Together Again*. Greenwich, CT: Fawcett, 1971.

[2]S. L. Bem, "The Measurement of Psychological Androgyny," *Journal of Consulting and Clinical Psychology*, 42, 1974, pp. 155–162.

Chapter V

HOW WE INVALIDATE ESP ABILITIES

So far we have seen that most of us choose an evolved life over death. As invisible creative beings who own bodies, I suspect that conscious evolution is only possible as we give more attention to our fundamental essence. As we move into consciousness of our spiritual/psychic/creative selves there will be an even greater need to take personal responsibility in our lives. We can no longer "let George do it" and, in fact, if we expect to move forward in our evolution together it will now be necessary for "each one to teach one." Evolution thus far has concentrated on biological forms, but now it is imperative to focus on the full scope of our abilities, both sensory and intuitive. Therefore, we can look at the word "responsibility" as "a response to our abilities."

Paranormal events have been carefully investigated by eminent researchers for over a hundred years all over the world. Yet, despite the technological advancements of our age, parapsychological research seems to be traveling at a snail's pace in the U.S. There are many reasons for this, including a lack of formal education for human evolution researchers and parapsychologists; limited funds for research; few scientists working full time in this area; and the fact that most of the work being done minimizes, mystifies, and mutilates the abilities of those who enter the laboratories. They minimize the abilities by concentrating on smaller and smaller details concerning them and then reporting them as statistics. The phenomena are mystified by the scientists by the obscure language and statistics used to describe them.

It is common knowledge among parapsychologists that when talented ESP specialists enter a laboratory and become "subjects," a decline effect is apparent in their demonstrations of ESP. There have been many articles and discussions about the "extinction paradigm," in which ESP abilities under strict laboratory controls are often extinguished.

The Fear Factor

These kinds of research problems are many and serious. The experimenters are wary of their critics and possibly unconsciously afraid of ESP abilities themselves. Exploring the unknown is a frightening business. This is especially true for those who choose to investigate large-scale psi phenomena outside the laboratory. To statistically determine if psychological variables such as spatial manipulation or absorption is more important to the out-of-body experience is a more popular research approach than to determine if there are energy patterns in and around the body and across space, when the person reports being out of body and actually gives some evidence that this was so by affecting an object at a distance or perceiving objects outside of the physical body's visual range. Out-of-body researchers today are focused on psychological theories of the phenomena instead of using technological equipment to search for an external component, such as energy patterns. If they are trying to prove it is all in the mind, why do they persist in labeling it *out-of-body experience*? One reason they don't take the bolder approach to their studies is that such a position might adversely affect their funding.

Researchers seem reluctant, especially in the presence of "critics," to discuss any phenomena comparable to that reported by the early researchers, for example the work with physical mediums Eusapia Palladino, Margery, and Eva C. They seem to be beset with what British author Brian Inglis calls "retrocognitive dissonance" in even looking back at the early phenomena. This means researchers rarely have faith in work that went on before because they weren't there and they don't trust early methodology. A verse that best describes this mistrust goes:

We were not there when it was found,
It therefore makes no sense.
Since we were not there,
It was not there
And it cannot be evidence.

For fear of sometimes uninformed critics, parapsychologists have sometimes thrown out the baby with the bath water. This resistance is historically consistent with the development of other emerging sciences. For example, in psychology: When the study was called demonology, all mental disorders were cases of possession; when it became medical psychology, mental disorders were no longer deemed to be results of possession.

The Parapsychological Association (PA), as a group, seems to look askance at independent researchers who want to examine massive phenomena, whether it be energy patterns around an out-of-body experience, large-scale psychokinesis such as moving objects, or hauntings and poltergeist studies. When former PA president Charles Honorton successfully captured a PK demonstration on film in which Felicia Parise mentally moved small objects, it seemed to receive less attention from top-level U.S. parapsychologists than Nina Kulagina's PK demonstrations some 10,000 safe miles away in the U.S.S.R.

Some researchers wanted Parise to repeat the phenomenon again and again, having little or no idea of the physical effort she had to make. She reported that she lost 15 pounds in the first few weeks of demonstrating her PK ability, and that it drained her of strength. Nonetheless, she moved small medicine bottles several inches, moved several corks, pieces of tinfoil, and a compass needle under a 15-pound glass bell jar while being filmed. She also moved a compass needle approximately 15 degrees in a laboratory, and while doing so, exposed film in opaque envelopes between herself and the compass, giving some notion of the pattern of the energy. Parise spent months getting her ability into visible operation and control, with a real motivation toward scientific advancement. But she eventually became burned out and discouraged by repeatedly having to demonstrate her abilities, more for the sake of curiosity than for critical scientific investigation.

When parapsychologist Gertrude Schmeidler[1] found that Ingo Swann's PK demonstrations produced temperature changes in the laboratory, and that she was able to measure these changes under controlled conditions with sophisticated instrumentation, she was not given financial support to refine her methodology and pursue this important finding. Other versions of the work with less talented PK operators were done, but the initial success was not retested.

Harold Puthoff's[2] measurements of PK changes by Swann on a shielded magnetometer at Stanford University were acknowledged, but, again, no attempts at replication or clarification of the first dramatic results were made. There were also somewhat invalidating reactions to Erlendur Haraldsson's and Karlis Osis's[3] reports of physical manifestations they witnessed with Sai Baba in India. Why are phenomena rejected when they present themselves in dramatic ways?

Parapsychologists worry about critics, but it seems they might take into consideration how hypercritical they are of each other. They are the "skeptics," remember, who have dedicated their lives to investigation of these matters. Those who question parapsychological findings without doing their homework might be more correctly identified not as skeptics, but rather as obstructionists.

So, why is parapsychology famous for the "extinction paradigm"? One possibility is that a researcher may be afraid of ESP phenomena but either not know this or not admit it. Repressed fear may manifest itself through defense mechanisms of denial and rationalization. If any massive phenomena occur, one might find ways of explaining it away as artifact, deny it outright, or simply not be able to see it. While all this is going on, parapsychologists intellectualize about the search for a repeatable phenomenon. If they suppress the occurrence of ESP in the first place for their own comfort, it is highly unlikely it will happen a second or third time in their presence.

Parapsychologists need to ask themselves if they are investigating ESP phenomena or suppressing it. If they are suppressing phenomena—because they are the people in the best position to do so—why are they doing that? They need to question why they are not getting more information from massive phenomena when it presents itself. The original psychic researchers made their impact on society chiefly because they had each other's support in doing the work as accurately as possible and in stating their opinions about their observations. There should be a similar sense of solidarity among parapsychologists today.

We all have a right to be afraid as we enter unknown regions of human potential, but forming networks to offer advice and support would facilitate the work and remove stress from individual researchers so that they could more efficiently investigate massive phenomena. Parapsychology could truly be the most important science of the future. However, if it continues on its present path, I suspect it will be supplanted by traditional scientists who are interested in conscious evolution and who possess the vision and courage to delve deeply into the multidimensionality of human experience.

Resistance to ESP Phenomena

Each of us suppresses ESP phenomena in one way or another. At this crucial evolutionary stage, we are timid about breaking through to a possible reality where our abilities can operate independently of the body, transcending time and space. We are on the edge of a leap in consciousness that would frighten anyone who became aware of it. We seem to be more afraid of the potential range of human consciousness than of blowing ourselves to smithereens. Work on "Star Wars" technology is funded in the billions and it progresses rapidly. Laboratories investigating expanded human potential in this country produce very little.

Researcher Charles Tart reported in 1978 that there were thirteen parapsychological labs in this country. Total funding over the previous five years was $552,000. Budgets ranged from $0 to $150,000 per lab. The average yearly budget was $42,000. However, the median budget was $17,000, so half of the labs got less than that per year to carry on their work. He also reported at that time that Soviets were spending from $20 million to $100 million a year for similar research. In 1986, it was suspected that the U.S. was spending $1.5 to $2 million per year.

British parapsychologist K. J. Batcheldor conducted group experiments attempting to document table levitation.[4] In these experiments, people sat around a table and tried to get it to rise off the floor without their physical assistance. While doing these studies, he came up with several psychological theories as to how the group members suppressed the phenomena. These theories seem to hold true for other experimental situations, as well as daily life observations of ESP phenomena. He says that although one could argue that phenomena which evade verification have no objective reality, it is also possible for a class of phenomena to exist that disappear as soon as one attempts to verify them by altering their surrounding conditions.

This is not only true of ostensible paranormal events. He relates an example from psychology. It seems that, one day, some of Pavlov's students had established some delicate conditioned reflexes in the lab dogs and wishing to demonstrate these to Pavlov, called him into the lab. To their dismay, the reflexes could not be elicited! In modern psychological laboratories this effect is so well known that special precautions are taken to exclude strangers from the room during conditioning experiments of this type. A person is a powerful "stimulus" in a lab and can upset the balance of the significant sensory input when delicate behavior is to be elicited. Novel apparatus can also have the same effect.

While mental ESP phenomena (telepathy, clairvoyance, and precognition) can be thought of as a form of human behavior, we do not usually think of table levitation as behavior. However, if we could begin to see it as an exceptional form of human behavior, we wouldn't be surprised to find that it is sensitive to critical observation.

Here are some of the interesting behaviors Batcheldor discovered among those who seek to observe massive phenomena:

1. Those who were sitting at the table that was to be levitated sometimes showed signs of resistance to being identified as a primary source of these strange happenings. He calls this "ownership resistance."
2. Resistance is sometimes shown to merely witnessing large-scale phenomena. He calls this "witness inhibition."
3. Both types of resistance tend to show themselves indirectly rather than as manifest apprehension, much the same as psychoanalytic resistance.
4. Both types of resistance tend to interfere with progress.
5. In such groups one person is often made the "scapegoat." At first he or she may be accused of pushing the table. Later, he or she may come to be regarded as "the medium." This relieves everyone else of responsibility.

Why do we resist so strenuously—whether it be a scientist in a laboratory who minimizes abilities by only reporting them as statistics, or an individual who refers to ESP experiences as uncanny, coincidental, or freakish? For one reason, it is safer to view experiences in these ways because if you try to convince someone you actually knew an event was going to take place and it did, they may think you are "crazy." Think about the reaction you would receive if you told someone you actually saw a table levitate and that you might even have facilitated it with your own personal energy.

Psychiatric/Psychological Duress

It is a fact that people are being labeled and institutionalized today for answering yes to such questions as: Do you sometimes think you pick up the thoughts of others? Do you sometimes think you can broadcast your thoughts to others? Have you ever had an experience in which you thought you were somewhere other than in your own body? Do you sometimes think you know about something that is happening even though you have no actual knowledge of it? Do you ever think you know what will happen in the future?

It is no wonder we cannot talk freely about our ESP experiences in an attempt to understand them when there are authority figures in the community who might feel obligated to use such information to jeopardize our freedom.

Today we have organizations such as the Spiritual Emergence Network that helps people understand new concepts of reality acquired through ESP and spiritual experiences. Helpers are volunteering all over the country, and we now have qualified counselors working with individuals who are experiencing conscious evolutionary growth.

But what of the scientific community? If a serious scientist reports that plants seem to respond to human emotions, his findings would probably be "dismissed" from any future serious consideration by his colleagues. Peer pressure and prejudice against the unknown can suppress valid experiences. Peer pressure can be especially disastrous if one is already experiencing a nagging concern about possible self-delusion. Observation of large-scale phenomena may throw one into confusion about long-held concepts of reality. It seems that if we are to take this evolutionary step that is before us, we will need to do it responsibly—and together.

Courage is the ability to confront whatever one can imagine. We appear to be a little short on courage right now because evidence for the existence of ESP in this society is more frequently obtained through dreams than in the waking state. In other words, it's O.K. to talk about a dream you had that seemed to indicate something might happen in the future. It's pretty safe—you were asleep, and it might happen sometime. Although this type of ability might appear to be the most difficult to verify, through the admirable work of Louisa Rhine and her colleagues, it has been ascertained that precognitive dreaming is the most prevalent of all ESP experiences.

We have another way of guarding ourselves against knowledge of our abilities. In ESP testing, results are compared to what would be expected by chance. If chance is six right answers out of 36 and you guess 12 right, you score significantly in a "hitting" direction. However, in our society, most results appear in a "missing" direction. It is as significant to get 1 out of 36 as it is to get 12 because it is a 6-point deviation from chance either way. If you tell test participants their scores are significant in a missing direction, it is easier for them to negate their abilities. Their resistance is often shown here by refusing to understand what you mean no matter how you try to paraphrase the fact that they achieved ESP success.

In this chapter I have pointed out just a few of the subtle ways we invalidate our abilities. We need to accept our extended sensory abilities and respond to them positively. Taking personal responsibility for claiming your extended abilities may not be easy; however, if you remain alert to your potential and have the courage and desire to develop and respond to your abilities, your life will be filled with new meaning and adventure. Greater understanding, appreciation, and actualization of your multidimensional self brings exciting rewards beyond the limits of your present creative imagination.

Chapter 5
End Notes

[1]G. R. Schmeidler, "PK Effects upon Continuously Recorded Temperature," *Journal of the American Society for Psychical Research*, 67, 1973, pp. 325–340.

[2]H. E. Puthoff, Stanford Research Institute research letter, dated June 17, 1972.

[3]E. Haraldsson & K. Osis, "The Appearance and Disappearance of Objects in the Presence of Sri Sathya Sai Baba," *Journal of the American Society of Psychical Research*, 71, 1977, pp. 33–43.

[4]K. J. Batcheldor, "Contributions to the Theory of PK Induction from Sitter-Group Work," *Journal of the American Society for Psychical Research*, 78, 1984, pp. 105–122.

Chapter VI

IS RELIGION HOLDING US BACK?

Many books, articles, and unsolicited letters are currently coming out of the New Christian Right (NCR), or fundamentalist movement, that are extremely critical of "psi phenomena." These writers seem opposed to anything "occult" (unrevealed) and depend largely on threats of Satan and Hell to marshal funds for their expanding operations. I went to church regularly as a young woman and was first introduced to spiritual ideas in fundamentalist churches.

The most basic and recurring themes of almost all religions are that: (1) we have a soul; and (2) we live after this life. I have always been interested in these two ideas, and my life work as a religious scientist has been to explore these ideas in depth and in the laboratory. Two other things that mainly interested me were the transformation of personality after conversion experiences, and the testimonies of those who witnessed the power of God in their everyday lives. These ideas and experiences have always been totally significant to my concept of myself. Therefore, a discussion of scriptures that suggest the expanded human abilities of Jesus seems relevant to this volume. Even in Jesus' time, the scribes, Pharisees and their followers, sometimes considered Jesus to be an instrument of the devil.

In this book we are exploring those things in our society that might serve as blocks to our conscious evolution. In many cases the teachings of organized religion that we are bound to the flesh and that identifies us as worthless sinners not only wrack us with guilt, they also limit our conception of ourselves as invisible, creative beings, both lowering our self-esteem and hampering effective living.

It appears from the various biographies of Jesus that he kept encouraging his students to have an inner experience of faith, in their divine inheritances, from the source from which all the good in their lives would flow. As a fully evolved human being, one with his creator, and with access to expanded human as well as co-creator abilities, Jesus will be the example for our own evolutionary process in this chapter. Our purpose here is to find out more about this elusive inner experience, with leads to an ever-evolving and expanding life.

The Purpose of the Gospels

The gospels were written long after the death of Jesus and after the Epistles of Paul had been in circulation for ten to fifteen years. This was unfortunate for growth of Christianity because it is possible that many of the actual teachings of Jesus (admitting that his virtual existence is still in question in many minds) were lost. The early Church doctrines focused on Paul's interpretation of those teachings, which he had on hearsay, having never seen Jesus.

In order to gain a well-rounded picture of the life of Jesus and his teachings, it is important to study each of the four gospels quite thoroughly. Each biography has its own character and point of view, according to the individual author. A different aspect of Jesus' life seems to have appealed to each of them. Yet in spite of the variations, our knowledge of Jesus is greatly increased by having the four different viewpoints.

The Gospel According to St. Matthew is the first book of the New Testament and is often ascribed to Matthew the publican, a tax collector and disciple of Jesus. However, biblical scholars believe a written piece by the disciple Matthew was used as the basis for the writing of this gospel. They attribute its authentic authorship to an anonymous theologian who lived in Palestine as late as 95 A.D. This is believed to be the approximate date that the gospel was written and the disciple Matthew had been dead for many years. Albert Williams' *The Book by My Side*[1] states that this gospel was written for the Jews in an effort to prove that Jesus was the Hebrew Messiah.

The metaphysical meaning of the name Matthew is "the will factor." Our will or intention controls, directs, teaches, and disciplines the faculties of mind. As one withdraws from focusing attention solely on mercenary occupations and material ambitions, there will be more time and attention applied to understanding invisible reality. Matthew, the disciple, a man of considerable wealth, willingly gave up his concentration on material existence and followed Jesus to learn more about spiritual realities.

The Gospel According to St. Mark was the first biography to be written after Jesus' death, around 70 A.D. Mark was a young man when Jesus was crucified and he later traveled extensively with the apostles Peter and Paul. Although he did not have a great literary talent, his book is straightforward and emphasizes the human aspects of Jesus. Mark probably wrote at least the first eight chapters of this gospel for early Christians in order to show them that Jesus was also human and had to face life on the same terms they did. Scriptures concerning the crucifixion describe Jesus' ultimate overcoming of bodily death. Such passages show that there is power within each of us to overcome adversity if we will only let it operate through us. Yet, these scriptures are sometimes misinterpreted in a manner that indicates we must suffer and be humiliated in order to receive grace.

The Gospel According to St. Luke was written by a man of culture, learning, wide intellectual appetites, and genuine literary abilities. Luke was the "beloved physician," companion to Paul, and probably a native of Greece. His gospel was written around the same time as the Gospel According to St. Matthew.

Luke wrote his gospel to be used as a legal defense for Paul at his trial in Rome. He was trying to prove that Christianity was friendly to Rome and that its followers had no intention of attempting to overthrow the government. He portrays Jesus as a gentle teacher with a profound interest in the poor and never as a political agitator.

Metaphysically, Luke represents the illumined healing intelligence in each of us, ever seeking to teach us more about natural laws and how to be in cooperation with them for our health and well-being.

The Gospel According to St. John—often called the "spiritual gospel"—is the fourth and last. The real author is unknown, but the work appears to have been written between 95 and 115 A.D. This book was written to show what the spirit of God can do through one person. It is a philosophic and metaphysical view of Jesus as a spiritual being. It was written to prove that *God is*. The writer portrays Jesus as the light of the world. He was explaining spiritual ideas that he knew would attract the attention of Greeks, especially philosophers and intellectuals. He was interested in gentiles accepting Christian ideas. He was trying to show that intellect is not the light, but rather the witness to the light.

In the West we hear so much about Zen Buddhism and Yoga in terms of spiritual enlightenment and growth. The teachings of Jesus are seldom found in volumes concerned with these topics; Christian mystics are rarely mentioned.

Jesus was born during a period when the Jewish people were undergoing tremendous persecution because of their religious beliefs. They clung to the expectation that a messiah would be sent by God to deliver them from their trials. Jesus was born a Jew and grew up in the devoted practice of Judaism, but because of his intimate knowledge of the universality of God, he attempted to reveal the nature of God to a wider congregation than those who regularly went to synagogues. He perceived that the necessity for a strict adherence to the letter of the law of Moses would alienate most gentiles. The farthest Jesus is reported to have traveled during his 3-year ministry as presented in the gospels was approximately 100 miles from his birthplace. He tried to teach, comfort, aid, and heal spiritually hungry people of various races and nationalities, including women. He, like other liberal rabbis of his time, attempted to subordinate formal worship to an inner spiritual communion with God.

Expanded Human Abilities in the Life of Jesus

The life of Jesus is a powerful demonstration of expanded human consciousness. The miracles, the healings, the tests and trials experienced and transcended by this man stand as a testament to the power of fully evolved human consciousness ever-connected to the universal source.

Many of the underlying themes of expanded human abilities studied by parapsychologists today are presented here as abilities that Jesus consistently demonstrated. For instance, most researchers agree that ESP data conflicts with a linear notion of time and space; in fact, ESP abilities transcend space-time barriers.

The first premise of ESP data is that there is a unity of all things and that a sense of oneness is key to the demonstration of these abilities. We shall see how Jesus taught his disciples over and over how to experience this oneness. It is a state of mind anyone can achieve. As an invisible truth, it first must be grasped in the abstract, and then be experimented with before one can be convinced of its reality.

Consciousness of access to everything through oneness provides a channel through which we can gain information across time and space. As one's intuitive ability is activated in this dimension, one begins to suspect that there are other alternate ways of obtaining information other than through the five senses. Such experiences allow us to see through the illusions and false assumptions under which we are presently operating. Evil becomes an illusion that can be seen as a lack of good. As negative thought patterns change and bring us out of the misconception of lack into the fullness of life—habits and behavior also change, showing us that the falseness of evil can be revealed and transcended.

Within the biographical accounts of Jesus, we see him using ESP abilities as a natural part of his teaching and healing ministry. We see him exercising telepathy, clairvoyance, precognition, and psychokinesis naturally.

Consider the gospels' recurring themes of:

- The oneness of all life.
- The ability to transcend time and space.
- The illusory nature of evil and lack.
- The ability to gain information from channels beyond the five senses.

These issues are important not only in the life of Jesus; they form the underlying reality waiting to be expressed through the lives of all those who strive to be fully evolved.

Jesus practiced the same abilities that today are deemed the "work of the devil" by many fundamentalists. Let's look at some examples of Jesus' expanded human abilities and see how they relate to our lives.

Jesus and ESP Abilities

Belief in the possibility of nonlinear time is gaining more and more acceptance as we move toward the 21st century. And yet precognitive individuals are condemned by members of fundamentalist religions as occultists. This is especially baffling when one considers that some of the best prophecies ever reported are contained in the Bible. The first of Jesus' miracles—his changing water into wine at the wedding party in Cana (John 2:3–11)[2]—might be explained today as psychokinesis.

Jesus often attracted great attention by reporting past, present, and future events in a person's life. For example, telepathy, or clairvoyance, is evident in the story of the woman at the well in John 4:7–30.

Jesus was in the process of teaching a Samaritan woman about the spirit of God and said to her, "'Go, call your husband to come here.' The woman answered him, 'I have no husband.' Jesus said to her, 'You are right in saying, "I have no husband"; for you have had five husbands, and he whom you now have is not your husband; this you said truly.' The woman said to him, 'Sir, I perceive that you are a prophet.'"

She listened to his instruction, left her water jar, and went to gather others to him by saying, "Come, see a man who told me all that I ever did. Can this be the Christ?"

The prophetic approach facilitated Jesus' teaching, and he became the wayshower to many by redefining the ways and teachings of the prophets and presenting them in the language of then current lifestyles. Jesus did not come into the world to abolish the old teachings, as he was sometimes accused of doing. He came to clarify, redefine, and extend the teachings.

Oneness; Universal Access: No Separation

It would seem the purpose of religion or spirituality is to make us aware of our unity with God. "Peace that passes understanding" comes to one who experiences his or her own beingness and recognizes the direct relationship with and connectedness to the universe. This peace cannot come by proxy—we have to realize it for ourselves individually.

One of the main ideas Jesus taught was that direct relationship with God was available to each and every one of us, just as he enjoyed it. We read his words in John 14:10–12, "... the Father who dwells in me does his works. Believe me that I am in the Father and the Father is in me. . . . he who believes in me will also do the works that I do; and greater works than these will he do."

There are dramatic examples in the scriptures of the oneness of the universe. For instance, as Jesus was being crucified, the veil of the Holy of Holies in the great temple in Jerusalem, which secreted the mystery of the Ark of the Covenant, was torn from top to bottom (Matt. 27:51). It appears this was done to show the people that there was no "being" behind the curtain, but that the Holy of Holies was available to all. Jesus advocated that people have a personal relationship with God, that all of us have access to this ultimate source.

This would also be another way of viewing his communion with his disciples at the last supper. Jesus told them to take the bread and wine and consider it as his body and blood. He then emphasized the idea that now I am in you and you are in me and we are one with God. The word "communion" means mutual participation and sharing. He wanted them to have their own personal, direct relationship with God. When he told them he was the vine and they were the branches, it was a message of power, love, and joy through connectedness, which thereby glorified God. When I reread these passages, I find it impossible to think of God as a separate male entity far away somewhere. To me, *God is*; therefore I am. There is no separation.

Did Jesus have any instruction in these matters or were his teachings purely inspiration from God? There can be no question that he was a scholar of the Old Testament and many think it is possible that he was versed in Eastern religion and philosophy. Some of his parables appear to actually paraphrase Buddhist teaching tales, for instance. It is believed by some historians that Hillel, the greatest rabbi of the time, chose Jesus as his student. The very fact that he was chosen by Hillel shows the great potential that was evident in the young man. Much of what Jesus taught came from Hillel; for instance, the idea that human beings are one and should act accordingly.

Hillel also advised against false pride, and taught that the person sitting at the foot of a table was equal to the person sitting at the head. In the gospels, Jesus often spoke of those who were first becoming last and the least becoming the greatest. He washed his disciples' feet to demonstrate that the master can be the servant and vice versa. He taught about the dangers inherent in discriminating between individuals based on physical characteristics or nationality or position—again, the illusion that we are sepaate. The parable of the good Samaritan (Luke 10:30–37) is an actual example of this philosophy in action, because Samaritans were discriminated against in Judea.

The "golden rule" was another teaching of Hillel's, and it is repeated in each gospel that we should love one another as ourselves (Matt. 7:12; Mark 12:31; Luke 6:31; John 13:34). It is unusual to find this sort of consistency in Jesus' teachings in the scriptures, which serves to stress the importance of this idea. Jesus taught a new commandment: Love thy neighbor as thyself. (Mark 12:29–31). He also advocated love of one God with all your heart, soul, mind, and strength.

Loving one's neighbors includes sharing our experiences with them. This is still difficult to do in this society, but as we erase ideas of fear and negativity from our lives, this intimate sharing will become more pronounced. By demonstrations of our faith, we set examples for our peers to follow. "Now faith is the assurance of things hoped for, the conviction of things not seen" (Hebrews 11:1). One thing we know about ESP is if we *believe* in it, it works better for us. Faith is like that. We cannot see our oneness with our eyes, but we can move toward it steadily by believing it is so.

In the sermon on the mount, Jesus told his followers, "You are the light of the world. A city set on a hill cannot be hid. Nor do men light a lamp and put it under a bushel, but on a stand, and it gives light to all in the house. Let your light so shine before men, that they may see your good works and give glory to your Father who is in heaven" (Matt. 5:14–16). This seems to be a clear statement that human beings are to realize their potential and express their abilities as a means of sharing that which they are.

While encouraging people to share with one another, Jesus found it necessary to advise his disciples against fanaticism, telling them that if people did not heed their teachings, no revenge was to be taken. Instead, they should quietly leave that place, shaking off the dust from their feet as they went (Luke 9:5).

There was a gentle caring in the way Jesus taught that we would do well to emulate. If a sinner is one who made a mistake. Through conscious intent or ignorance, Jesus' instruction was to repent, i.e., to turn around and stop making that mistake. Then all was forgiven. The simplicity of the message almost makes it seem incredible.

It is unwise to try to force our ideas on others, and if we attempt to teach what we perceive as truth and it is not well received, it is wise to go calmly on our way undisturbed, unprejudiced, and noncombative, while retaining our conviction of our personal truth. Each one of us experiences the logical and exact result of our own receptivity.

Through improper sharing we can actually create an appearance of separation. Our own faith might be damaged if sharing is not done in the gentle, caring manner of our example, the fully evolved Jesus. In Matt. 7:6, Jesus warns, "Do not give dogs what is holy; and do not throw your pearls before swine, lest they trample them underfoot and turn to attack you." Sometimes we might become so overjoyed with the knowledge we are receiving of our oneness with spirit and our access to all things, that we want to share it enthusiastically with others. Yet, if they are not receptive to these ideas, they may argue with us, contradict us, or even try to destroy our faith. It behooves us to share our knowledge, but not to try to convince those who oppose us. This is very important to learn in the practice of metaphysics as well as in fundamentalism, for Jesus said, "He who has ears, let him hear" (Matt. 13:9 and 43).

Our self-knowingness is the incarnation of our potential. We might consider ourselves ideas seeking to become operational in one infinite mind. Each person could be considered an individualized center of one consciousness. Jesus perceived this when he stated, "I and the Father are one" (John 10:30). We cannot separate ourselves from universal energy, intelligence, or substance if we perceive this universe as a unity. Jung set forth this unified theory as the "collective consciousness." It is possible that as we think, we set the creative mind into action. We can draw from infinite life that which we envision it to be, and so, truly, it is done unto us as we believe.

Illusions of Lack, Evil, Limitation, and Space-Time Barriers

The primary illusion that stifles human beings and blocks their self-expression is the idea that we lack what we want or need in our lives. This illusion is shown in the following example.

Several of Jesus' disciples were fishing one day and complaining bitterly about catching no fish. Jesus told them, "Cast the net on the right side of the boat, and you will find some" (John 21:6). When they made this change, they could hardly pull in their nets because they were so full. Fish represent spiritual ideas in which there is great possibility of increase. Sometimes we are so resistant to change or to accepting grace that we continue to use an idea that obviously isn't working to our advantage (fishing off the left side of the boat). We get into automatic habits, which require some thought and effort to change.

However, as we consciously evolve, if we are willing to work with new ideas and change our habits, as well as our self-image, we can experience an abundant life. The disciples had continued to concentrate on the emptiness of the sea and complain about no fish—negative. Jesus acknowledged that there were no fish where the nets were presently, but he went on to seek a solution by offering an alternative—positive.

Another example of this teaching is found in John 7:24 when Jesus said, "Judge not by appearance"—appearance of lack is an illusion. If you want something—whatever it might be—and it appears impossible to achieve it by all logical reasoning, stop intellectualizing your problem. Don't concentrate on the impossibility, but keep a clear picture of the end result, however irrational it may seem. Don't take anyone's word about the efficacy of this principle, do your own experimenting. Concentrate on your desire, imagine yourself as being it or having it, believe that it is so and expect to realize its physical manifestation.

Focus on the desired result and "Keep your eye single" (Matt. 6:22–23). Don't let self-doubt and ideas of limitation distract your mind with apparent reasons why it can't happen to you. Even as you are aware of how the present appears to you, focus on the desired end result. If you place your attention and belief on obstacles and perceived possible ways to overcome them (even though you know you don't know how), it's like planting a seed and then leaving town. You reap what you sow *and* tend.

Concentrating on our desires, rather than the lack of our desires, will eventually lead us out of lack into the fullness of life. One may be criticized as a passive idealist, but to practice the principles that underlie the ideal and thereby bring it into manifestation is an achievement to be admired and imitated.

There was no lack where Jesus was because he lived in abundance in his consciousness. In Matt. 14:13–21, Jesus fed over 5,000 people with five loaves of bread and two fish. The loaves might represent spiritual substance and the fish, spirit itself. He separated the food into small pieces and gave them to his disciples who in turn gave them to the people. Everyone ate and then Jesus told the disciples to collect the leftover food. They gathered twelve baskets of scraps. On another occasion, 4,000 people were fed and seven baskets of meat were left. By gathering up the fragments, the disciples were given a powerful lesson in that they experienced and acknowledged the multiplication of substance.

Jesus spoke of this kind of sharing when he sent his disciples off to preach, "Heal the sick, raise the dead, cleanse lepers, cast out demons. You received without pay, give without pay" (Matt. 10:8). This directive applies to us today as we expand our human abilities to improve the world condition. There are people who pretend to have ESP abilities and healing powers when all they have is an expanded gift of gab. They are exploiting people to improve, not the world, but their own financial condition, which often seems to be in a shambles. Allowing yourself to be deceived by charlatans will not advance you in your personal evolution.

In Matt. 25:14–30, Jesus relates the parable of the talents. We all have talents but they must be used if they are to be beneficially increased and multiplied. It is the responsibility of each individual to find his or her own talents, develop them and use them to increase knowledge and joy in our environment. You cannot hide or ignore your talents and expect them to reap any rewards. It is by using them that your talents and abilities are translated into prosperity. If they lie dormant, there is no wealth—if they are expressed adequately, they can be translated to substance. Looked at from this perspective, you are money to the extent you will translate your abilities into form. Suppressing or repressing inspiration can leave us somewhat lifeless, because it takes a lot of energy to hold in abeyance one's expanded human abilities. If you are afraid to express yourself because of low self-esteem, you may not find your innate potential.

The servants in the parable who exercised faith and went out and traded their talents, doubled the amount they possessed. The servant who was afraid and buried his talent, lost even the one he had when the master returned. They all had equal opportunity to increase that which was given, but two had faith and one was afraid. I take this to be what Jesus meant when he said, "I tell you, that to every one who has [faith] will more be given; but from him who has not [faith], even what he has will be taken away" (Luke 19:26).

Neglect of the body and the belief that we must be poor and unhappy are contrary to the teachings of Jesus. If poverty and prosperity are two ends of the same law of demonstration, we need to consciously move toward the end that feels more comfortable for us. Otherwise, our lives just happen to us, and we complain and moan and can't possibly experience the joy of successful living. Your success lies at your point of interest. If you want to be on subsistence payments because you don't want to take a job, realize that and enjoy it to the best of your ability. If you want to be rich and famous and can withstand the pressures of such a life, go for it! Success is in your heart, not in your surroundings. Any idea that denies our divine birthright—that we are created in the image and likeness of God—is an immature conception of the self. Jesus said, "I came that they may have life, and have it abundantly" (John 10:10). We affirm lack with ease, but plenty with some difficulty; thus we are moving ourselves toward lack in the midst of plenty.

Just as we can focus on lack, we can focus on fear and evil. Fear is the opposite of faith, and evil could be thought of as the lack of good. Experiencing fear and evil is somewhat like going into a dark room and dreading what may lurk there. If you don't know where the light switch is or how to turn the light on, you may stumble and hurt yourself. Once you know about the light, however, there is no need to fear the darkness.

In the parable of the vineyard (Matt. 20:1–16), Jesus was saying that no matter what our previous experience, when the time comes that we actually do change from destructive to constructive thoughts and actions, everything is ready to receive us and work with us. The workers who were hired at the eleventh hour received the same pay as those who worked all day. We also see this in the story of the return of the prodigal son (Luke 15:11–32). When he came home, they celebrated his return to the dismay of the son who had been there all along. When we turn toward the good, at whatever hour, it is ready to pour itself out on us. What some consider evil, condemnation, or judgment, others consider only appearances with no reality base.

We all know how difficult it is to deal with temptation, whether it be the temptation of fearful and obsessive thinking or the temptation to act against our ethics. During Lent, many people fast and refrain from eating or drinking some substance. I challenge you to fast from temptation on a mental and physical level. How did Jesus, fully evolved being, resist temptation and stay on course?

One scripture tells us that he fasted forty days in the desert and his instruction was "... that your fasting may not be seen by men but by your Father who is in secret" (Matt. 6:17–19). This teaching, when considered metaphysically, may show how one can select a positive idea and then surround it with so much negativity that the positive goal fades away. When you know what you want, it seems necessary to fast from negativism so that the idea you want to materialize isn't eaten up. The main reason for fasting from the negative appears to be so the positive can express itself.

While fasting these forty days in the desert, it is written that the tempter or devil came to Jesus to divert him from his purpose. Matt. 4:4, 7, 10 indicates that Jesus never uttered one original word to the tempter, he merely repeated scriptures, and thus stood firm in his faith and teachings. He didn't belittle his opponent or become defensive. Temptation had no power against this sense of purpose. The devil departed and angels came to comfort and strengthen Jesus. Shortly thereafter, he left the desert and went to Galilee to gather his disciples and begin his ministry.

How many times have we had a sincere purpose for doing good and then been tempted to depart from it? If we have been tempted away, then we need to search out our motivation behind the idea in the beginning. Becoming conscious of our motivations is a major evolutionary step. Sometimes we may do something that has the appearance of a generous act when it is really a manipulative one; or good deeds may be done for the purpose of ego satisfaction. If our motivation is to do the will of God as a way of life, and if we keep focused in this determination, temptations will decrease. I understand "doing the will of God" as going within and seeking knowledge of my purpose for being on this planet and then acting on that knowledge. Many people say they don't know what they want to do, but a vigorous internal search will reveal what one is to do. The rewards of doing the will of God far surpass any material gains. Living in the will affords its own joy, power, and abundance.

In your efforts to expand your human abilities and evolve consciously, belief is essential. You will have to take things on faith in the beginning until you experiment with invisible reality and begin to see your belief demonstrated at the material level. Jesus taught us to believe that as we pray, we have already received. Prayer accepts its own answer as an image in the mind before invisible energies can play on it and make it manifest. Our prayers should neither be bargains with God nor seek to deprive others of their highest good. If we are conscientious about our personal ethics, the law of cause and effect will grant us what we can accept. We are more receptive as we expand our conscious perceptions of the abundance of life.

Jesus knew that people were often burdened with guilt over past mistakes, so he sometimes found it necessary to assure them that their past mistakes were forgiven, so they could accept the healing or prospering word. Consider your actions carefully in the present, and guilt will be a thing of the past. If you do make a mistake, you can apologize and forgive yourself. This will relieve guilt feelings, which could be unconscious blocks to a richer, fuller life. Pray for those who use you spitefully—that is what Jesus taught.

If you want to become a fully evolved conscious being, self-condemnation is always destructive to your aim. Try not to indulge in this self-punishment. We have all done things that were not for the best, but these things may have been done out of ignorance of our true nature. The universe holds nothing against us, no matter how many mistakes we make. As we turn away from our destructive thoughts and actions, they are forgiven us and we need to forgive ourselves. If we are sincere in our efforts at spiritual growth and conscious evolution, the rewards will be great in terms of increased self-expression and physical demonstrations of our faith. Try to learn to forgive yourself completely and quickly because ignorance of the law excuses no one from its effects. You are cooperating with natural laws every day, whether you know it or not. Bring yourself to the awareness of this invisible reality.

When Jesus raised his friend Lazarus from the dead (John 11:1–44), he demonstrated the reawakening of spiritual ideas. We often become buried in negative beliefs. As we become consciously aware of this state, we can begin to "roll away the stone" of negativity and awaken the sleeping consciousness of youthful vigor, enthusiasm, spontaneity, and creativity.

Jesus spoke about maintaining a child-like approach to the world. It has also been suggested by various parapsychologists that ESP is more of a primary process function. It seems to have characteristics similar to prelogical or child-like thinking. There is a tendency, for instance, to identify one aspect of an ESP target at a time as it appears. Responses are more about details than the totality or the meaning of the presentation. Some scriptures advocate child-like faith and absolute trust. In Matt. 18:3–4, Jesus describes conversion as becoming as a child. Child-like belief and acceptance of the operation of natural principles is one path to happy demonstration of that belief. Jesus also said, "let the children come to me and do not hinder them; for to such belongs the kingdom of God" (Luke 18:16). When we believe as we did as children, we may find it easier to let go of ego demands and allow ourselves to receive wisdom and the gifts of the spirit. We will no longer be compelling a reluctant force.

The Healing Principle

One form of expanded human abilities is spiritual healing. This ability also requires a child-like approach, for in mental healing we believe that what we have thought will actually take form in our lives and the lives of those about whom we are thinking. The simplicity of the technique almost precludes one's knowing that by thinking or imaging we can set a principle into operation that may cause a healing process to take place in someone's physical body. Spiritual healing is the conscious use of the healing principle for the purpose of helping those who are sick or in need. Jesus demonstrated this principle on many occasions and told his disciples that they, too, could do all these things and more. We also have access to this healing principle. The more we practice working with it, the more readily it works for us. The more we believe in and participate in the healing principle, the less we are affected by suggestions or conditioning that reinforce the idea of inevitable illness.

Jesus understood his spiritual nature and spoke from that center rather than from limited consciousness. Through his example, he showed us how to become fully evolved human beings. He reiterated that the same spirit is within each of us, and as we recognize this, we harmonize with the good, and with truth and beauty. When we learn to think with focus and calm, while realizing the tremendous power to which we have access, we can expect to bring expanded experiences into our lives.

When Jesus healed the centurion's servant at a distance, he said, "...be it done for you as you have believed" (Matt. 8:13). In this healing, Jesus showed (Luke 7:2–10) that if we have a firm belief or inner knowing, we don't have to be at the same physical location of another person to effect spiritual healing. One of the fundamental concepts of conscious evolution is that time and space can be transcended and that we can operate independently from our bodies. These concepts are verified by over a hundred years of ESP research. The time has come to reconsider the assumption that we are limited by linear space-time barriers. By recognizing the perfect spiritual being of a person, changes can be manifested in the physical body. If our realization of the perfection of our spiritual selves becomes a subjective embodiment, healing can take place.

"Miracles" of the Disciples

In John 14:12, Jesus told his disciples that they could do all the things he had done, and even greater things, because they all had the same access to spiritual principles. And they did! In the extreme case of death, Peter raised Tabitha (Acts 4:40–41) and Paul affirmed life in Eutychus (Acts 20:9–12). The apostles cured people of fever and dysentery (Acts 28:8–9), and cured the lame (Acts 3:6–8). Ananias cured Paul's blindness (Acts 9:17–18), and Paul refused to be affected by a poisonous snake fastened on his hand (Acts 28:3–6). Apostles were miraculously delivered from prison (Acts 5:18–19), and Peter was also delivered out of chains and prison (Acts 12:7–11). Jesus' statement probably applies to humanity today, and we can use it, if we will know it and accept it. Any "miracle" that Jesus or the disciples performed can be accomplished through us as we reach their evolved state of consciousness. By reading these stories in the original, you can start to get a sense of your own tremendous human potential.

Paul especially advocated that we recognize within us what he called "Christ consciousness": "So if there is any encouragement in Christ, any incentive to love, any participation in the spirit, any affection and sympathy, complete my joy by being of the same mind, having the same love, being in full accord and of one mind" (Phil. 2:1–2). Miraculous power and grace can operate through us as we arrive at this state of expanded consciousness. (There is an excellent definition of grace as it relates to ESP in M. Scott Peck's *The Road Less Traveled.*[3])

People who witnessed the miracles of the disciples experienced a variety of reactions and effects. Today, people have similar reactions to ESP demonstrations. Public opinion could be totally reversed in the face of such miracles, which was also true of Batcheldor's witnesses of table levitation (see pages 110–111). For example, in the case of Paul with the snake, witnesses first said, "No doubt this man is a murderer," but when Paul suffered no harm, they "changed their minds and said that he was a god." With Batcheldor's witnesses, first a person at the table was accused of manipulating it (the scapegoat), and later was declared the "medium" or cause of the phenomenon. Opinions based on outward appearances can often be misleading.

Some witnesses were amazed and confounded; they marveled; they were filled with wonder and it threw them into doubt. Some were afraid of the power they witnessed, astonished; some bowed down in worship and praise and glorified God; some received conviction or belief. Many clung to their denial of such things. It is said about them that "their hearts were hardened."

Today we hear a great deal about hardened arteries (arteriosclerosis) that block the veins within the heart. It is almost fashionable to have a bypass operation and detour around the hardened heart. If denial is your major mode of psychological defense, reconsider its effects on the body. If you often hear yourself saying, "I can't believe that," "No way," "Never," "It can't be," and such statements, then denial may be your chosen method of self-defense.

It is possible to ask questions of anyone, get facts, weigh evidence, and draw conclusions about any topic, no matter how frightening or intimidating. There is an alternative to negative resistance. The Lord said to Joshua, "Be strong and of good courage; be not frightened, neither be dismayed; for the Lord your God is with you wherever you go" (Joshua 1:9). Some of the witnesses to miracles asked many questions of the healee and family and friends, while others advised that no one speak of "this thing that we have seen."

Jesus' Humanity

We sometimes get so caught up in the divinity of Jesus that it is difficult to relate to him as a fellow human being. However, he is portrayed in the gospels as human as you and I—physically, mentally, emotionally, and spiritually. When he heard that his friend Lazarus was dead, he was deeply moved and wept (John 11:35). When he was hungry and found a fig tree that bore no fruit, he cursed it, and it withered away (Matt. 21:18–19). If someone performed psychokinesis in this manner today, some would call them "workers of evil" or worse. When Jesus entered the temple on two separate occasions, he became enraged with the buying and selling, and he made a whip of cords and drove out the robbers and money changers (John 2:14–16). We see power being exercised over the televangelists today and recall the saying that "God will not be mocked."

Jesus' potential nature seems to have been similar to ours, but his knowledge of it was enlightened and actualized. He understood universal access and he had complete reliance on spiritual principles. We have the same access to the principles he taught, but we do not have the same reliance on them. We need to learn to acquire this reliance, no matter how much time and effort it takes. Comprehending universal access expands our knowledge base and propels us to evolve consciously.

We have within ourselves the key to freedom, but until we learn to use it consciously, our lives follow uncertain patterns. The subconscious mind will create for one as easily as another, but we have to supply the pattern for its creation. You can't build a house without a blueprint, unless you are willing to settle for an unstable structure.

Ideas firmly planted—or buried—in the subconscious mind tend to manifest themselves as real life situations.

An analogy for our unconscious mind might be the Earth itself. It does what it does without regard for how it does it. Our conscious mind is like the gardener who decides what to plant, nurtures growth, and harvests the crops. Once we put the seeds in, we don't have to tell the Earth what to do; it knows its part. If one plants carrots, the Earth cannot choose to yield potatoes. With this image in mind, think joy instead of sorrow, abundance instead of lack, and life instead of death.

Practical Idealism

Most of us tend to dismiss idealists as unrealistic dreamers who don't have a chance of ever making anything important happen. But in Webster's dictionary *idealism* is defined as: "a theory that ultimate reality lies in a realm transcending phenomena; a theory that the essential nature of reality lies in the consciousness . . ."

The life of Jesus is of particular value in our study of the evolutionary process because Jesus was a *practical idealist*. He was able to demonstrate the ultimate invisible reality to people so they could learn to use it for themselves and others. Jesus was a revolutionary in terms of conscious evolution. It has taken us 2,000 years to even consider his life in these terms, let alone try to *emulate* the standard he set for us both as individuals and as co-creators.

The teachings of Jesus are practical techniques for

effective daily living. Jesus knew that he was surrounded by infinite wisdom and substance. He recommended that each of us come to this realization for ourselves. He taught that we are inlets to all knowledge, and as individuals we become outlets insofar as we can get distortions in our personalities and egos out of the way and allow ourselves to know and become.

Principles can do nothing for individuals until they are made specific and used. As we grasp these principles, we need to practice them consciously and clearly, understanding their operation and expected results. The principle of intelligence can be experienced as direct knowing or intuitive guidance when we accept and use it. Prayers are answered on the level of the mentality of the one praying, and each person receives as much guidance as he or she is capable of perceiving.

Jesus stressed the importance of keeping your focus on your own spiritual growth rather than finding fault with others. This is the essence of the scripture, "Why do you see the speck that is in your brother's eye, but do not notice the log that is in your own eye?" (Luke 6:41). He called those who did this hypocrites and suggested that if they concentrate on their own spiritual growth, they will then be able to bring forth good in themselves and others. Spiritual growth and conscious evolution are synonymous. Applying the principles of the scriptures can be one way to develop the attitudes prerequisite to expanded human abilities.

Jesus took religion out of the temple and into one's heart, when he said, "God is spirit, and those who worship him must worship in spirit and truth" (John 4:24). When we function in spirit and truth, there is no need for loyalty to a building, a person, or a creed. Fellowship with those who understand these principles *is* necessary. It helps us keep our faith strong by witnessing the workings of spirit in our own lives and each other's. As we become conscious of a universal power greater than we are, we start to know and feel it impelling us toward wholeness. We begin to understand that we are more than we appear to be; that potential is unlimited in each of us. As we accept and express this potential, our appearance and behavior change.

Natural laws (i.e., spiritual principles) are in operation right where we are at any given time. It is our responsibility to learn how to cooperate with them. For instance, the invisible law of gravity holds each of us on the planet regardless of race, creed, color, sex, or social standing, as long as we don't put on antigravity boots. Our thinking is attracting whatever we concentrate on most into our physical lives right now. If we are obsessed with ideas of fear and disease, we experience them. If we focus on love, health, wealth, and self-expression, we get that.

We can only know that which we experience through our thinking and feeling nature. Theory can never satisfy as much as demonstration. We shall know God when we have a sense of it within our own being. Yet a change of consciousness does not come by simply willing or wishing. It is not easy to mentally embrace an ideal of harmony while experiencing human discord, but it is possible.

Money as a Tool for Conscious Evolution

When we begin to understand our divine nature, we find there are four primary areas in which we become confused and may suffer. These areas are: love, health, wealth, and self-expression.

One idea that causes a great deal of confusion is that being wealthy is a hindrance to conscious evolution. We have given too much significance to the idea of money, which is only one form of substance with which we have daily contact. One tends to accept substance in the form of food, clothing, and shelter, but we more often hear people complain of lack of money.

Jesus found no fault with riches and usually stayed at the finest homes when he entered a town, but he taught that one should not make money the goal, that it was not an end but a beginning.

Most people don't love money, they love the freedom that having money gives. Money frees us to do all sorts of things: it enables us to learn and to better ourselves in various ways; it gives us time to consider spiritual and social concerns; it allows us to help others. Conscious evolution demands that we change our concept of money as a form of substance separate from the abundant substance of God. There is only *one* substance regardless of the many forms it takes. Money, as one proof of God's substance, is available to us at all times no matter what our paycheck looks like.

Jesus often spoke about giving and receiving, and we see his instructions on reciprocity in all the gospels. Luke 6:37–38 makes it clear: "...give, and it will be given to you; good measure, pressed down, shaken together, running over, will be put into your lap. For the measure you give will be the measure you get back." A "weekly" wage doesn't compare to "abundant life."

Jesus knew the story from II Kings 4:1–7 about the woman who could get as much oil as she could accept when she followed the prophet Elisha's instructions. A widow came to Elisha and told him her husband was dead and that a creditor had come to take her two sons to be his slaves.

"What shall I do?" Elisha asked. "How much food do you have in the house?"

"Nothing at all, except a jar of olive oil," she replied.

"Then borrow many pots and pans from your friends and neighbors!" he instructed. "Go into your house with your sons and shut the door behind you. Then pour olive oil from your jar into the pots and pans, setting them aside as they are filled!"

Her sons brought the pots and pans to her, and she

filled one after another. Soon every container was full to the brim!

"Bring me another jar," she said to her sons.

"There aren't any more!" they told her. And then the oil stopped flowing.

When she told Elisha what had happened, he said to her, "Go and sell the oil and pay your debt, and there will be enough money left for you and your sons to live on."

The moral of this tale is that prosperity will come as you evolve consciously. You have to make room for your prosperity to come to you. It cannot flow into a vacuum—no more jars; no more oil. But if you make a place for prosperity in your life, it will appear in increasing amounts.

Obsession with money, whether worrying about its lack or how to get more, is a counter-evolutionary state of mind. It is not until we recognize our union with all aspects of the universal source that we begin to grasp the meaning of prosperity—unlimited substance—and we can begin to have a healthy money consciousness.

Money is a good place to practice the shift from ideas of lack and limitation to those of connectedness with infinite source. Universal substance is always available in invisible form and able to provide us with everything we need in any form we choose.

Singleness of Purpose

It is only as we integrate our thinking and feeling natures and take necessary actions on our ideas that we begin to demonstrate our expanded human abilities. Scribes and Pharisees stood on street corners and intellectualized about religion, but they didn't have the feeling (Matt. 5:20). Luke 22:38–52 discusses the false beliefs of the Pharisees and lawyers and how they hindered others from entering into knowledge.

We hear a lot of talk today about the second coming and how things will be in the millennium. But *right now* is the time to begin to become the person you were created to be. In Luke 17:20–21, the Pharisees asked Jesus when the Kingdom of God was coming. He answered, "The kingdom of God is not coming with signs to be observed; nor will they say, 'Lo, here it is!' or 'There!' for behold the kingdom of God is in the midst of you."

As far as I can ascertain, the "Kingdom of God" is an indwelling presence, a "state of consciousness" in which a being is in harmony with its creator or source. As we expand our consciousness to consider faith as the point of knowing that the universe withholds no good from us, we can understand the statement, "It is your father's good pleasure to give you the kingdom" (Luke 12:32).

It is relatively easy to think about these ideas or discuss life principles intellectually, but those who internalize them to the extent of feeling and sharing them, know meaning, purpose, and fulfillment. They experience this "kingdom" in terms of increased happiness, joy, or a heavenly or blissful state of being (Matt. 5:19). If we turn our attention to our innate potential, we will experience these states of being more often and for longer periods.

Sometimes we have to garner our thoughts like a shepherd tending sheep. If a sheep goes astray, it is brought back to the fold with care and attention. We need to watch and tend our thoughts in a similar manner. "The eye is the lamp of the body. So, if your eye is sound, your whole body will be full of light" (Matt. 6:22). Our eye is sound as we perceive the unity of good. When we practice this "singleness of purpose," we are provided with externals that are necessary to our personal well-being. Increased certainty in the efficacy of conscious evolutionary principles allows us to have no fear of tomorrow, to enjoy today, and to refuse to dwell on the mistakes of yesterday.

We cannot guide others if we are in darkness or ignorance. First we clarify our own vision, then we become as lights, lighting the way for others. We cannot cooperate with invisible reality until the light of knowing clears away the darkness of our confusion. Reexamine any personal assumptions that come to your attention to see if they are still viable in your present life.

In this "enlightened" age, we see sickness and deprivation running rampant in our world. It is somewhat of a mystery why we adamantly refuse to accept the facts of universal principles underlying our world. If we could accept invisible reality and begin to experiment with it from the point of view that we are creative beings who own bodies, but have the ability to operate on invisible levels, we could use these principles to great advantage to bring some order to the chaos we see all around us. As long as we continue to view ourselves as "mere mortals," our innate potential will be lost to us. Can we afford such a loss?

Chapter 6
End Notes

[1]Albert N. Williams, *The Book by My Side* (New York: Duell, Sloan & Pearce, 1963).

[2]All scriptures are taken from the Revised Standard Version of the *Holy Bible*. New York: Thomas Nelson & Sons, Old Testament Section, 1952, New Testament Section, 1946.

[3]M. Scott Peck, *The Road Less Traveled* (New York: Touchstone, 1978), pp. 235-312.

Chapter VII

ARE WE HOLDING OURSELVES BACK?

Within the evolutionary process, we move from self-awareness to self-knowledge to self-actualization. In this chapter, the self represents your unrestricted potential, or if you prefer, that part of God which is you. Try not to think of yourself as a one-dimensional being, a product of a certain cultural background, restricted to your genes and your environment, but as someone far more multidimensional —whom you are seeking to be aware of, know about, and express in your daily life.

In the allegory of the Garden of Eden, human beings were thrown out of the garden because they became aware of good and evil. This gave them the right to choose—free will—but it also excluded them from eternal life—the immortality of their God-like selves. Most people experience limited free will, but the further along one moves in the evolutionary process, the more the exercise of free will expands and increases our ability to create and control our own realities.

We hear a lot today about freedom and responsibility, but we hear little about the tremendous courage required to make these qualities effective in our lives. One has to be quite bold to actualize their potential. Others may not understand you or may criticize you for your unorthodox behavior. Conscious evolution requires that you give yourself permission to be unorthodox, but not unethical. Moral responsibility and ethical behavior depend on self-awareness.

Conscious Friendship

Friendship is extremely important in the process of becoming aware of expanded human abilities. We sometimes think we are afraid to get close to others; we may be afraid to let others know who we are, because of our unconscious sense of inadequacy. When we are misunderstood in childhood, we dissociate from what is going on and become people pleasers with multiple personalities in order to stay safe. Fear separates us from the self.

Interaction between friends increases awareness in each of them. You may lose your center or personal identity with an erotic lover or even in a purely social setting, but friendship allows people to find their true selves in each other, and supports greater self-knowledge and self-actualization. One of the special rewards of friendship is the mutual discovery of unknown potentialities for understanding. We allow ourselves to move away from our ego toward friends as we show concern for them. One of the principles of human affinity is that when we do this, we benefit from the act of concern for another. Friendships are mutually beneficial out of concern for one another, and this is the shared beauty and happiness we experience. Friendships encourage and support expanded consciousness.

Many of us are incapable of meeting the demands on self a friendship brings. We are content with superficial interactions that require little of us. Here is where laziness can be a major stumbling block to evolutionary progress. It requires some effort to get close to others, but true friends pay attention to one another. They are continually exploring and probing each other in the attempt to make each one more complete through drawing out the secrets of another's being. Each one intuitively recognizes that the potential of the other is unlimited, and they help each other break down the walls imposed by self-limitations.

They are seldom completely satisfied with the friend's progress, but consistently urge them on to greater spiritual understanding and growth. Spiritual understanding in this sense is helping the friend to become aware of his or her potential to know more and more about possibilities, and ultimately to get those ideas operational so that all may enjoy the uniqueness of that special person.

Friends live for one another in a sense. It may seem more devastating to lose a close friend through death than to die oneself. Self-sacrifice is one of the more demanding criteria of true friendship that leads many to be satisfied with less intimate relationships. In a conscious friendship, both parties have so much to gain—and lose—that few people seem truly willing to take the risks involved. J. Glenn Gray, a veteran of World War II, says in his book *The Warriors*[1] that "only the slow, unpredictable development of conscientiousness and concern for others brings us close to them, not mere acquaintance and surface intercourse, not mere knowledge." As Eldridge Cleaver wrote in *Soul on Ice*,[2] "What an awesome feeling it is to be on the verge of the possibility of actually knowing another person."

Change is still abhorrent to most of us even though we are in the midst of tremendous societal change at this point in our evolution and are faced daily with astonishing risks. Staying flexible is essential for mental and emotional survival at this stage of human evolution. Transformation of personality, which may include loss of ego, should be expected. The rewards for not holding onto ego are great and can open one to realizations that may initially boggle the mind. But such realizations can be understood and actualized through disciplined inquiry and patience.

Conscious evolution in terms of one's mental life may involve a search for knowledge. However, integrating this knowledge into one's physical life requires translating it into action, even though one's emotional life may still seem to be a battle for mere survival. In this case, our flight-or-fight instincts may start adrenalin roaring through our systems even when all we are confronting is an emotional conflict. This confusion causes unnecessary wear and tear on the body. And because of the emotional confusion, one may lose sight of mental clarity. Emotional immaturity and insecurity causes us to abuse our bodies, our minds, and probably our very beings.

We try to forgive ourselves for not knowing how to handle certain emotional challenges, but we wouldn't have to forgive ourselves if we wouldn't condemn ourselves in the first place for not knowing.

Self-Condemnation

One of the most insidious obstacles to conscious evolution is self-condemnation. The personal distrust that fuels this negative spiral can be considered one of our most serious mental illnesses. To be told by religious leaders that all humans are born in sin and will eternally fall short of the glory of God does not enhance our personal growth and spiritual actualization. What's the use of trying to evolve to embrace our God-self if our innermost self keeps suggesting to us that we are irreparably flawed.

As we try to define ourselves in this way, someone

may be in our environment who is unaware of their own feelings of shame and he or she may tell us we are selfish, ugly, or worse—no good. Unaware that this behavior is harmful, we may then pick up and unconsciously carry their shame. When we try to regain our self-esteem and assert ourselves, we may be told we are belligerent, rebellious, or too aggressive. More shame. When we report our thoughts and feelings to those closest to us, again because of their own shame, they sometimes tell us we shouldn't think or feel "that way." Out of their denial of their own emotional state, they may imply we are stupid or ridiculous. More shame.

Once we are totally ashamed of our true selves and our personalities are distorted beyond recognition, what difference does it make what we do? At this point, ideas of right and wrong have no impact on our behavior. All we started out to do was to become the best version of who we are, but on the way, we've gotten totally off the track.

Yet, these ideas of low self-esteem and worthlessness contribute nothing toward further manifestation of our innate potential. In fact, they tear down and destroy any attempts at personal evolution. Could it be that preachers keep announcing that we are sinners because without sinners they might be out of business? Could it be that members of our family find our way of being and seeing threatening to their acceptance of low self-esteem? All rigid authority figures are using the same natural laws to produce what they need in their lives that are used by those who seek expanded consciousness. Both sides know the power of the spoken word. If one needs to control bodies, one needs to diminish consciousness. Our evolutionary aim, however, is to bring more and more of our human experience to consciousness.

I don't believe I get better by asking myself "What's wrong with me?" The distortions of the personality are largely camouflage. What I want to know is "What's right with me?" and let my behavior catch up with this inner knowing. If I focus on what is wrong, my behavior will reflect that as I see it. I want to be aware of that within me that knows, that can, that loves. As I let my intuition lead me to this knowing, I can then allow it to express through my behavior. I find it best to keep these ideas as simple as I can. I don't know how to fix the distortions in my personality, but I do know how to get in touch with my inner being.

As we begin to know ourselves more thoroughly and come out of denial, we may find dark and ugly places within, which will have to be lightened up and aired out through recognition and acknowledgment. Confession may be helpful in this process. We will also find radiant places within. Unfortunately, some people, including clergy, psychologists, and psychiatrists, look for the dark and ugly places in order to exploit the confused human being.

If we expand our awareness to perceive sin as a mistake based on lack of knowledge, we can see that each of us has indeed sinned. But as we experience the error of our ways and become more in tune with our true nature and purpose, we will be less likely to make these kinds of mistakes. It will become evident that this behavior is harmful to us as well as to others, and we will begin to change our behavior.

Resentment and Revenge

Another harmful thinking pattern is harboring resentment or seeking revenge. These are major blocks to our conscious evolution, as well as to our mental health. Angry feelings harm us physically, mentally, emotionally, and spiritually. If I insult my neighbor, I may feel guilty about it and my emotions begin to work against me. Although it may feel good in the moment, ultimately there is no satisfaction in invalidating or belittling others. This is not to say that anger is not sometimes appropriate, but it is possible to find ways of expressing it without hurting yourself or others.

We are moving toward the ideal of Godhood through the power of love, which is the connective energy of all things in the universe. We are moving toward the idea of unity through cooperation and understanding. Condemning ourselves or each other is not God-like and therefore is out of phase with our forward movement. Such derisive behavior causes friction, which ultimately destroys if it is not noticed and corrected. As we move forward in our conscious evolution, we are going to have to move obstacles out of our way or get around them. We are going to have to stay on track and not be discouraged by delay or confusion or be tempted to go off on first one tangent and then another.

If a point of friction becomes apparent through a relationship or misconception, we are either going to have to correct it or move away from it. Choices such as this require courage and discipline, but nobody suggested that becoming more conscious was going to be easy. It may be easy to sit in meditation and "be still and know that I am God." However, maintaining that attitude in daily life is somewhat more difficult. An optimist once said, "the difficult we do immediately; the impossible takes a little longer." So keep a sense of humor to release tension, and keep your eye fixed on your spiritual goal.

Potential Genius

To become aware of our potential, knowledgeable about it, and able to get it actualized will require at the very least, serious self-examination. I was surprised to learn in my reading and searching that the first definition of the word genius in Webster's dictionary is "an attendant spirit of a person." Other definitions, in order, are: "a strong leaning or inclination"; "a peculiar, distinctive, or identifying character or spirit"; "a personification or embodiment, especially of a quality or condition"; "an elemental spirit"; and as a fifth definition: "a) a single, strongly marked capacity or aptitude, b) extraordinary intellectual power especially as manifested in creative activity, c) a person endowed with transcendent mental superiority; specifically, a person with a very high intelligence quotient." Inspired by this new information, I began seeking knowledge of my own personal genius. I thought I'd better check a thesaurus to make sure I wasn't confused, and once again the first synonym was "spirit."

So maybe it *wasn't* my "potential" I was after. *Roget's Thesaurus* listed potential as an adjective meaning "dynamic, magnetic, charged; dormant, latent; unfulfilled, promising." Perhaps it may be more correct to think in terms of potential genius. Potential can be used as a noun, as something that can develop or become actual, but the idea of seeking the attendant spirit of myself or my elemental spirit appealed to me.

I read about Thoreau, who was considered a genius by naturalist and anthropologist Loren Eiseley in his book, *The Mind as Nature.* Thoreau led a solitary life that led to intense self-examination. He said, "I have the habit of attention to such excess that my senses get no rest, but suffer from a constant strain." Eiseley said about Thoreau: "... in this supremely heightened consciousness of genius the mind *demands* expression. The spirit literally cannot remain within itself. It will talk if it talks on paper only to itself, as in the case of Thoreau."[3]

Breaking Down Barriers

There are barriers between conscious and unconscious levels of thought, as well as the obvious barriers between intuitive and logical thought that will have to be transcended to arrive at our innate potential genius and the freedom to create or actualize that particular genius. In other words, our freedom is increased to the extent that we can gain access to our true selves.

An analogy might be the plight of disabled persons. When architectural barriers—narrow doorways and lack of ramps impeding wheelchair movement, etc.—prevent disabled people from entering and participating in "normal" life, society sees something wrong with these people. Today, as some of these barriers are being removed and all people are being given access to institutions, corporations, auditoriums, and natural wonders, we begin to see that something was wrong with our architectural planning. If normal-sized people had to use the furniture in a dwarf's home, they might think there was something wrong with the furniture, but if they saw the dwarf climbing onto their furniture, they might think there was something wrong with the dwarf. Access is the key word here—it breaks down barriers.

What we can gain access to as a physical being might be called organic opportunity—analogous to the architectural access described above. Eiseley believes that organic opportunity has placed sharp limits on a far greater life potential than is ever permitted to enter the actual world. Expression of one's genetic or personal genius "becomes frightfully obscured by the environmental complexities which surround the birth and development of the individual."[4]

Speaking of acknowledged geniuses of our time, Eiseley writes:

> Sometimes they are starved by poverty, self-schooled, sometimes they have appeared like comets across an age of violence. Or they have been selfless, they have been beautiful or unlovely of body, they have been rake and puritan. One thing alone they have in common: thought, music, art, transmissible but unique.[5]

Educators and scientists who are rigid, dogmatic, and arrogant about human experience are setting up unnecessary blocks before us as we try to move into a future reality. The acceleration of change we are experiencing at this moment in our conscious evolution defies such limited perspectives. We need self-awareness, not ego; flexibility to cope; and a sincere desire to know our individual potential genius and purpose. Those who go in search should understand that something new may emerge into consciousness and they will have to cope with it and elaborate on it for its best and fullest realization. There are risks to coming out of comfortable niches and ruts—you may never be the same again.

Some of us are born with spiritual genius. There are natural saints on the planet today, but most people find them a total mystery. Saints seem to be filled with knowledge and love of God from their earliest memory and are unsullied by the temptations of worldliness. It's difficult to believe there are such transcendent souls among us. Other saints have triumphed over great hardships and inner struggles in order to serve others.

However, the Indian philosopher Vivekananda in *How to Know God: The Yoga Aphorisms of Patanjal,* commented:

> Perfection is in every man's nature, only it is barred in and prevented from taking its proper course. If anyone can take the bar off, in rushes

> nature. . . .In man there is the potential god, kept in by the locks and bars of ignorance. When knowledge breaks these bars, the god becomes manifest.[6]

Vivekananda stresses the great importance of right environment and association with those who are spiritually minded as a very significant part of conscious evolution. Try to be with people who let you feel comfortable and uplifted. Watch out for people who do not contribute to your health and well-being. Behaviors one should be aware of in themselves or others include: lying, sarcasm, exploitation, manipulation, revenge seeking, deliberate baiting, piquing of jealousy, threatening, or coercing. There is always a reason if you are feeling uncomfortable, hurt, worried, disappointed, angry, jealous, or otherwise emotionally upset. If the only reason you can come up with is another person and you cannot make them aware of your uncomfortable feeling and its origin—get away from that person.

I have been around people with whom I felt so uncomfortable I would rather walk through a mine field at midnight than remain in their presence. Check out what is happening in your world when you feel serene, secure, and loving—surrounded by understanding, kindness, and support. These signals will show you which of your experiences are conducive to the expansion of your consciousness.

Denial of the Self

Many people in our society use alcohol and drugs to avoid facing reality and to have psychic and spiritual experiences. However, the use of such drugs promotes denial of all levels of reality and may even bring about a prolonged spiritual dryness and crisis of disbelief.

Individuals obsessed with fantasy on or with TV, sex, sports, cars, videos, clothes, and other people's lives may also find themselves living in a spiritual desert. Any of these are great places to hide if you want to avoid accidentally coming face to face with yourself. You've probably been pretty well convinced in this shame-based, consumer-oriented society that you won't measure up—so why look?

How are we to come out of self-denial? We deny there is anything wrong with us even as we feel the pangs of physical, mental, emotional and spiritual pain. We deny that we have access to the liberating power that can make us whole and complete in every aspect of our being. We deny we have desires, for fear they will not be fulfilled. We deny that we are interested or even enthusiastic about an idea, for fear we will have to become involved and spend time, energy, and effort to bring the idea to fruition. We restrain ourselves from positive action, for fear of being criticized. We may even be afraid to share the good of our lives for fear someone may try to take it away from us, make it seem less, or actually con us out of it. We unconsciously place limits and restrictions on everything we say and do.

If the perfection that is in each of us begins to manifest in all its abundance, we may think we are too manic, when what we are probably experiencing is enthusiastic joy and ecstasy. But how many of our peers can understand and share these feelings with us, much less support them? What we might do is rush off to get some drugs that will bring our mood down. It's perfectly O.K. to be depressed in this society, but its usually not O.K. to be ecstatic.

Even our societal psychological labels are oriented toward dis-ease. For example, consider such labels as: "learning disabilities" instead of "learning variations"; "personality disorders" instead of "multifaceted personalities." We know people who are accident prone, but what of the majority of us who are accident resistant? People are given negative labels by authority figures, and they have to live with those labels the rest of their lives if they do not feel adequate to reject the suggestions. Drugs, however, are given positive labels. I have been very bored and extremely enthusiastic, but I refuse to label myself manic-depressive in order to take less responsibility for the reality I create. I refuse to allow another person to place a label on me that will cause self-doubt and decrease my possibilities for self-knowledge and actualization.

Self-doubt robs us of the faith that allows us to cooperate freely with life's self-creating powers and therefore, our ability to actualize the infinite possibilities that lie hidden in our lives. Self-doubt can often lead to despair. Paradoxically, despair is the most frequent trigger of ecstatic experiences. And ecstasy has a transforming quality. The old sayings about the darkest hour being just before dawn or people's extremities being God's opportunities are seen to be true in this light. If you are feeling bad, try pushing it to lousy and even unbearable, because when you reach the bottom, there's no place to go but up. One could feel "bad" forever and depress all thoughts, feelings, and activities for a lifetime, but this is such a limiting experience. Why not get an idea of the full range of feelings, strengths, weaknesses, imagination, energy, and laziness in your personal life? Once you have a clearer idea of your range, you will have more freedom to move, experience, and express yourself. Limitations are generally self-imposed. Truth will set you free.

Growth Through Crisis

Pain and grief can be valuable motivators. Many people will not do much self-searching until they are sick, poverty-stricken, or institutionalized, when their pain and fear become motivating factors in seeking knowledge of their potential and purpose. For those who experience one crisis after another, unaware of their need to supply excitement and adrenalin rushes to which they may be addicted, there is hope. Improved self-observation can allow you to use even crises as opportunities for growth. Disorganization and destruction often precede change and development. If you find yourself in a crisis, try to observe your thoughts and feelings about what you are trying to get away from and where you would really like to be.

Although we are cautioned to avoid negative thinking, it is important to remember that our thinking is only negative when we "get stuck" in the illusion of being alone and not knowing. By using crisis as a mirror for seeing yourself, you can turn a negative situation into a positive opportunity. In this case, our negative thoughts, feelings, and self-image—which Carl Jung called our "shadow"—can sometimes be utilized as tools for self-discovery—as can seemingly negative events in our lives. By seeing these as creative challenges spurring our growth and universal understanding rather than believing we are victims of bad karma or capricious fate, we can take charge of our own lives.

Any of our unconscious human experiences that we can bring to consciousness will move us forward on our evolutionary path. This includes the powerful spiritual lessons inherent within our own and humankind's darker side. We must acknowledge, accept, understand, and forgive all aspects of human behavior—dark as well as light; our own as well as others'—if we are ever to achieve conscious evolution.

Conscious evolutionary "change" is sometimes frightening. It is somewhat like the process of extinguishing the ego to arrive at enlightenment in Buddhism. Monks and other adepts have to undergo extreme conditions, personal hardships and torturous trials to break through to enlightenment. It's much the same in critical everyday life changes. Robin Norwood, who wrote *Women Who Love Too Much*, had this to say about the process:

> Don't let the discomfort stop you. The fear of change, of relinquishing what we've always known and done and been, is what holds us back from our metamorphosis into a healthier, higher, more truly loving self.
>
> It is not the pain that holds us back. We're already enduring alarming levels of pain with no prospect of relief unless we change. What holds us back is the fear, fear of the unknown. The best way I know to confront and combat fear is to join forces with fellow travelers who are on the same journey. Find a support group of those others who have been where you are and who are headed for or have already arrived at the destination you want to reach. Join them on the path toward a new way of living.[7]

The Danger of Normality

If everything in your world is exactly as it should be, in your total control, comfortable and rewarding, you may be in a rut, and it may be time for some change. Transformation requires moving into the unknown, whereas conformity leaves us in the safety of the known. Conforming to the group, however, can rob us of our originality and potential genius.

Even more limiting than conforming to the group is the way we conform to ourselves and become self-satisfied. We may know that something we are doing is not exactly right, but "everybody does it." We might consider our indifference as nonjudgmental and virtuous. As Oscar Wilde pointed out, "a cynic may feel safe in knowing the cost of everything and the value of nothing." If you are afraid of being hurt, you need to know what is wrong in the world so that you can avoid it, as opposed to knowing what is right and moving toward it. There is no need for moral values in such a state of fear.

On the other hand, there are those who must make everything they do "perfect." Ideals of perfection also change, but few seem to notice this. For instance, something could be perfect in one stage of growth and equally perfect at its next, but different, stage of being. What is perfect for one person could be crude and imperfect to another. Therefore, perfection is transient or evanescent. People will often delay producing their talents or even refuse to express them outwardly because they "aren't quite right yet." They won't sing their songs, send manuscripts off, invite six people to dinner, fly solo, or show the love they feel in their hearts because it isn't "perfect" yet. We have such a short time to express life in our present physical forms, and yet too often we delay and stall as if we had an eternity.

Next, we have the person who refuses to act outside of established rules and regulations with practically no regard for how these arbitrary rules were established. Here we have the murderers of our planet who kill and maim because some authority figure ordered them to do so. Authority figures usually stay well behind the front lines. Nazis pushing Jews into ovens were merely following orders. Groups can do unconscionable things and deny any responsibility for their actions because they were "following orders."

If these actions were taken on individual volition, conscience could be a determining factor. In the words of Nietzsche, "Survival without integrity of conscience is worse than perishing outright." Martin Luther King spoke about the merits of longevity but added, "I would rather die tomorrow than live to eighty with a butchered conscience." Be courageous; act on what you know is good and true; and stay away from those who create unhealthy environments around themselves.

The rules and regulations people also stop the advancement of innovative ideas. It is easier to abide by the rule than try to change it. Those who settle for the easier way out to avoid effort or embarrassment do not often know the glory and exhilaration of successful living. When they see someone else's success, they may speak of how lucky that individual is. But I believe the more one applies oneself to one's own projects, the luckier one gets.

However, one can also conform to one's own ideas of worthlessness and emptiness. It is possible to prefer chaos, abuse, and confusion to one's own boredom. Some people think anything is better than having nothing at all happen day after day. If we could only make peace as exciting as war, maybe our planet would be moving permanently in a safer direction. Yet a peaceful spate often exposes a void in a person. Too often such voids are not filled with constructive thoughts and actions. The excitement of crisis, of rescuing oneself and others, seems natural to one brought up in dysfunctional surroundings where life was seen as a struggle to survive. To such a person, boredom may be more terrifying than life-threatening situations. To confront the reality of one's beingness and reflect on it could be dreadfully dull and senseless to one still in a survival frame of mind. It is only when survival is somewhat assured that the search for knowledge may begin. Physical life—survival without meaning—is not the highest good for conscious beings.

How can we make peace as exciting as war? How can we make people willing to lay down their lives for each other in the cause of peace and love as they do in war? Soldiers show a vast capacity for self-sacrifice in war, and it may be this particular aspect that makes war so fascinating for its participants. J. Glenn Gray noted that inhuman cruelty and superhuman kindness can exist simultaneously in the same person under the stress of battle. Here again we see the paradox of being pushed to the extreme in order to ask and listen for the answers to such simple questions as, "Who am I?" "Why am I here?" "What is my purpose in life?" As Gray says:

> The ways of peace have not found—perhaps cannot find—substitutes for the communal enthusiasms and ecstasies of war. Unless we find a way to change [people's] hearts, there appears to be small chance that they will fall out of love with destructive violence.[8]

Seeing Ourselves as Each Other

There is another state of being where one is content to simply observe some spectacle. For instance, some people will draw so close to a fight to watch the bloody brutality of it that they will completely ignore their proximity to danger. Others will stand out all night in bitter cold to watch a meteor shower or some other heavenly spectacle. They may feel giddy with certain sense of awe that they can observe the power and grandeur of an orderly universe. They can intellectually know the speed of our planet around the sun and within our galaxy, and yet feel very secure standing on top of the planet recognizing that they are an integral part of all that.

Once I was thrown off a motorcycle that was just taking off, going about five miles an hour, but I have no fear of being swept off the planet as long as the invisible force of gravity holds me in place within the speeding system traveling at tens of thousands of miles per hour. I am sustained and supported within my world, subordinate to it, but not separated from it.

However, there is something special and valuable about you and me within the solar system because so far we have only found five billion people such as ourselves who can know this universe exists. We have the unique gift of consciousness that allows us to move from self-awareness to knowledge to actualization. Human beings are the only ones on the planet who experience conscious evolution; we are the ones who can change our perceptions of this universe as we evolve.

We can agree, as a group, on any reality we choose. We can, for example, agree on a common self-image that will incorporate dignity, integrity, cooperation, and sharing through love so that those born on the planet will not die of starvation or ignorance, but will instead live to know their part in the total scheme of the universe and lead rich, fulfilled lives.

It is essential to move away from total self-interest in order to encompass this larger image of the unity of humanity. We will need not only to see ourselves as each other's keeper, but to be able to see ourselves as each other. There are many rewards connected with this realization. For example, to be outside oneself, beyond reason and self-control, is the definition of ecstasy. If we become consumed with curiosity it may result in self-forgetfulness; or awe might take us beyond the barriers of self; but ecstasy transcends both these states of being because it is a conscious experience of a power greater than ourselves with which we can merge completely and yet experience ourselves as parts of a whole.

Many people report that the idea of separation has no reality within the experience of ecstasy. All the defense mechanisms and barriers we have set up, consciously or unconsciously, to isolate and "protect" the self are seen as unnecessary and, in fact, impediments. As Gray writes:

> It is in moments like these that we feel rescued from the emptiness within us. In losing ourselves we gain a relationship to something greater than the self, and the foreign character of the surrounding world is drastically reduced....many have felt similar urgings toward the infinite in moments of extremity, and, though they cannot be articulate about such experiences, they are rarely quite the same afterward.[9]

The Language of the Heart

How can we regain our lost sense of unity without feeling deprived as individuals? For one thing, we can look for our similarities rather than our differences. We have been advised and educated in Western society to look for differences, being told that this is the proper way to approach data. This appears to be a distinctive "divide and conquer" message for reasons of power and greed. Many college-educated people might disagree with me, but the power of verbal language cannot be underestimated, and cultural brainwashing affects us all.

But there is another language in humankind's grasp—the language of the heart. Some people call it love. You don't hear very much about this language in the vast halls of higher learning, but it's something that seems to be a natural human capacity. When we tell someone how it felt when we were first in love, no matter how misguided it appeared at the time, we are speaking the language of the heart. Everyone who has experienced a first love will understand and empathize with at least some of the thoughts and feelings expressed. The experience of love helps us break through our illusion of separateness, and highlights our feelings of togetherness and union.

Love is expressed in many forms. Television is filled with pictures of winners from sports events to beauty pageants to game shows to entertainment award shows. We love to celebrate together the victory of others. That, too, is the language of the heart. Over 300 million people watched the last royal wedding on TV. They watched the blessing of God being called on to solidify the union of two people. It was an affirmation of our global unity that worldwide we were so interested in union and the family feeling.

There is a series on television called "Tales from the Dark Side," which shows sinister and bizarre behavior. If over 300 million people watch royal weddings and millions more watch the anniversary celebration of the Statue of Liberty, which stands for opportunity, equality, and sharing, isn't it possible that people might be more desirous of watching "Tales from the Light Side"?

Have you ever seen someone do something truly courageous and felt pride in that person's accomplishment? Remember that marvelous scene from the movie *Norma Rae* where the heroine is in the mill holding up the strike sign? I was moved to tears each time I saw it and finally realized exactly what was affecting me—IT IS WONDERFUL TO SEE PEOPLE MAKING A DECISION TO STAND UP FOR THEMSELVES! The language of the heart reaches through our differences to the essence of human experience in which we all share. It emphasizes our feelings of similarity and, therefore, our oneness.

There is a lot of concentration in this society on how to *give* love. There are books on unconditional love, instructions on how to show someone your love or give love to one's community. We are sometimes asked if our love is merely an addiction or even if it can happen after a certain age. Very seldom is there anything written on how to *receive* love. It's as if we assume that it's a natural instinct to receive love, but that we must be taught to give love.

There are also all sorts of data on how not to be bad, but very little data on how to be good and enjoy it. I believe we not only need to learn to receive love, we also need to learn how to enjoy success, and experience happiness. If one has grown up in surroundings that abuse the true self, one may have expected love from a parent who was incapable of demonstrating love or even of being trusted. Then, generally lacking trust in others as a result of this experience, we may be unable to feel or receive love from another. Our focus may be more on when the inevitable betrayal will occur. Spend a little time thinking about how you experience the love of another human being for you.

Another misunderstanding about love is that hate is its opposite. Love may take an active form or a passive form, such as well-timed empathy. In the active form, the opposite may well be feelings of hatred, but in the passive form, we may experience apathy as love's opposite. We may also think we understand the active form of love (sex, for instance), but the passive form is more elusive and subtle. Most love is probably expressed in the passive form, that is, being there for the beloved in every way—mentally, emotionally, spiritually, and physically.

It may be extremely difficult for some to receive the feeling of being loved passively. Try not to resist love from others. Try to experience it, and verbally acknowledge that you are receiving it when you feel it. Saying thank you for love received could make a world of difference in an intimate relationship. Try not to deny your own good feelings; share them, with discretion.

We are too often caught up in looking outside of ourselves for the truth of our being. We delude ourselves by thinking that if we only had a better job or more money or a good relationship or another child that everything would be all right. We examine what has influenced us in the past and want to know what we will be in the future. Everything of importance seems to be out there, or back there, or over there. That is how we miss the magical "now"—the experience of living in the moment. It's no wonder we find it difficult to cope when we are focused on other times, places, and things instead of compartmentalizing our attention to present experience.

It is our experience *as we know it* that is the fundamental truth of our being. We have been told by mystics and philosophers for centuries to "know ourselves." Our level of anxiety is often so acute it is almost impossible for most of us to be "be here now." The writer Thomas Carlyle wrote in the 19th century, "Our main business is not to see what lies dimly at a distance, but to do what lies clearly at hand." If we could practice this suggestion, it could reduce our worries and anxieties immeasurably. It is not necessary to require oneself to do this every moment of every day; gradual improvement is sufficient.

Many of us intuitively know the basic soundness of this principle, but we continue to worry and fret about first one thing and then another. We forget how crucial it is to an evolved life to be with oneself and know oneself in the moment. This kind of forgetfulness holds us back in our evolutionary process.

Chapter 7
End Notes

[1]J. Glenn Gray, *The Warriors*. New York: Harper & Row, 1970.

[2]Eldridge Cleaver, *Soul on Ice*. New York: McGraw-Hill, 1968.

[3]Loren Eiseley, *The Mind as Nature*. New York: Harper & Row, 1962, p. 48.

[4]*Ibid.*, p. 51.

[5]*Ibid.*, pp. 51–52.

[6]*How to Know God: The Yoga Aphorisms of Patanjali.* Hollywood, CA: Vedanta Press, 1962, pp. 204–205.

[7]Robin Norwood, *Women Who Love Too Much.* Los Angeles, CA: Tarcher, 1985, p. 276.

[8]Gray, *op. cit.*, p. 216.

[9]*Ibid.*, pp. 36-37, 39.

Chapter VIII

GET ANOTHER SELF-IMAGE

Conscious evolution involves the acceptance of your natural self—the individualized, uncompromised consciousness that incarnated on this planet to actualize its fullest potential. We are not merely descendants of apes or children of God. We are not merely cogs in the machinery of life grinding away as tools of production. We are not simply fluidic matter in motion. We are not just consumers programmed by the media to buy an endless array of products to make us better. We are multidimensional beings with a tremendous scope of abilities, which as yet remain largely untapped. We are currently poised on the brink of a totally different idea of reality.

As you begin to see beyond the illusion of space-time, and even past the barriers of physicality, your concept of reality will shift. You will begin to gain increasing knowledge of the self that is you and the purpose of your existence. Such knowledge will come from your expanded human abilities, not your intellect.

It is by gaining information and knowledge through your five senses, and your capacity for creative abilities that extend the range of the senses, that you begin to set the stage for your personal evolutionary process. Your role is to prepare for this tremendous growth surge through the conscious necessary purification of your body, mind, and emotions.

This type of activity cannot be confined to a linear time frame. Moments of insight and enlightenment may occur spontaneously and instantly, or take a lifetime of disciplined or unconscious pursuit. To have any expectations as to when events will happen in this process is somewhat defeating. It is better to simply acknowledge that your timing is perfect.

Through this intensive self-preparation your vision will be expanded and clarified. You will see more, and see it more clearly, in both the physical and nonphysical dimensions. The more clarity of vision we gain, the less willing we will be to allow distractions—whether they arise from personal relationships, work situations, financial woes, or the drain of ill health, all of which demand our attention.

It will take you to a point of readiness to act, and as you are poised at this point, you will receive additional knowledge and power from a source beyond yourself. No external obstacles can interfere with the process once it is at this stage—only you can.

Fear,
Unbridled ego gratification,
Denial, and/or
Profound feelings of inadequacy

all constitute elaborate forms of self-sabotage that we may employ, consciously or unconsciously, in order to resist our breakthrough to the expression of the evolved self.

Once we begin to actualize our true potential on a daily basis, we will no longer be living in regret of our past mistakes or be obsessed with a constant effort to improve our character. We need to stop judging ourselves so harshly and begin to understand, accept, and respond to our tremendous untapped abilities.

Your personal efforts to attain self-knowledge and actualization may not increase the quantity of your years but they will definitely improve the quality of your life. To live a life of fear is unacceptable to those who understand that they can actualize their faith and feel power, love, and connectedness. Although we may live in a threatening environment, if we expand our inner awareness, we can cultivate a calm, steady state of being, and we can be the cause of our experiences, rather than the victim of outward circumstances.

The threat of a nuclear winter hasn't been completely eradicated, but with *glasnost* the U.S.S.R. and the United States have never been closer to arms reduction. We don't have a cure for AIDS today, but the rampant homophobia and wholesale rejections of AIDS patients is becoming less and less acceptable in American society. Conscious evolution reminds us that reality is an agreed-on concept and that, as people continue to change their individual consciousness, group consciousness will shift and our world will be transformed. I praise each and every one of you who is daily attempting to work with your own personal vehicle of transformation. Each person who gains consciousness *is* making a difference, whether one knows it or not.

Conscious Evolution and Imminent Death

When people come to view themselves as creative beings with visible and invisible abilities, and feel O.K. about experiencing themselves as operating independent of their bodies, it may soften the impact of the many transitions we are going to witness in the coming years. The National Academy of Sciences predicts that starting in 1990, the disease AIDS will kill as many Americans each year as the Vietnam War killed in an entire decade. Death on a foreign shore can be denied, but it is not so easy in your neighborhoods and families. Young people, who consider themselves indestructible, will be less careful in their sexual practices —especially if they are under the influence of drugs or alcohol. The AIDS epidemic threatens young lives much more than mature, monogamous people.

Can we face this magnitude of death with our current self-image that we are mere bodies? Or will we have countless spirits clinging to the Earth, trying to express themselves through unsuspecting people?

Will the victims of AIDS and drug overdoses be able to realize they have lost their bodies at such a young age? One wonders if there will not be countless young spirits attempting to possess those who are less conscious because of laziness, drugs, or lack of knowledge. As the worst epidemic of medical history, these transitions are going to bring us face to face with situations beyond our imagination. Are we ready for such extraordinary circumstances in our present state of consciousness?

Can you imagine a worse hell than to be a bodiless spirit trying to communicate to a loved one in body and always being ignored? You have probably experienced at one time or another how painful it is when your physical presence is not acknowledged and you desperately need attention. If you die at a young age and don't know you lost your body and you try to communicate with the living and nobody sees you or recognizes your presence, you will know what it feels like to be punished.

What About Spirit Possession?

Many questions may arise as we move toward an expanded idea of what it means to be human. If our self-image is that of a creative, invisible being who owns a body, what if another spirit could somehow intrude, take over, or express itself through that body which we call ours? The idea of spirit possession, of the disembodied interfering with mortals, is not addressed by a majority of the members of the psychological community today. Before the advent of psychoanalysis, every disease that could not be explained by the male practitioners was considered a case of possession by demons. Holes were drilled in heads of patients to let demons out (trephining). As psychology sought to become an established science, the idea of demonology was thrown out along with *any* idea of possession as an actual cause for illness, addiction, or mental confusion. With current issues of death and dying, walk-ins, and spirit invasion, perhaps the idea of spirit possession must be reconsidered.

Bill Finch, who wrote *The Pendulum & Possession*[1] in 1971, thought that he had found a way to detect possession or interference and also a method of exorcising the intruding energy. He did not feel that all possessing entities were earthbound spirits or demons, but that some could be energy masses that remain after the physical body is destroyed. We have all experienced static electricity around our bodies in one way or another. One example is walking across a rug and receiving a shock when we grasp a metal doorknob.

Bodies are electrochemical systems, and many electrical devices have been invented to "cure" us of our ailments. Electroconvulsive shock therapy (ECT) is probably the extreme of this treatment theory. But does ECT rearrange brain cells or drive our possessing entities or energies, when a marked effect of the treatment is observed? Although Finch discusses these ideas, his own method is called "bioenergy exorcism" and uses only healthy, human energy to remove unwanted or possessing energies.

Fifty years earlier, Dr. Carl Wickland used electrical techniques and documented his research in his classic book, *Thirty Years Among the Dead*,[2] published in 1924. He was attempting to get other professionals to consider the possibility of invisible reality. Sir Arthur Conan Doyle said he never met anyone with such a wide experience in invisibles, adding, "No one interested in obsession or the curing of insanity by psychic means should miss this book."

On the one hand, Finch used a pendulum to diagnose, and a charismatic approach to exorcism. Wickland's wife, on the other hand, was a trance medium, and she greatly facilitated his work. When Wickland suspected possession, he passed a static electricity device over the patient's body to drive the spirit out of that body and into the body of his entranced wife. The spirit could then communicate through Mrs. Wickland and be helped on in its evolutionary process. The patients invariably showed signs of improvement. A patient's personality would sometimes be transformed to a remarkable extent, resulting in a much happier, healthier life. Addictions, illnesses, and paralysis could also be removed in some cases. Dr. Edith Fiore is one psychologist who treats possession, and her book *The Unquiet Dead* sheds some light on this phenomenon.

When I talk to sensitives in psychic communities across the country I hear of rescue work with earthbound spirits. I read of walk-ins, where a person agrees to let a disembodied spirit express itself through his or her body, and of takeovers, where a person is overpowered by a discarnate. Yet I remain mystified that there is little mention of such issues within the parapsychological community. Parapsychology, as a science, is still in such an infant stage of development that most parapsychologists are probably as frightened of being associated with ideas of possession as the early medical psychologists and their successors are to this day.

However, I believe that parapsychologists have the right, if not the responsibility, to examine these ideas, comment on the problems encountered, and suggest possible solutions. The investigation of matters that seem to be affecting thousands of humans at the present time would be a tremendous service to humanity. Psychology and psychiatry do not heal by labeling symptoms. Labels, in fact, are often conducive to the restriction of serious investigation and may sometimes adversely affect or even block a person's natural healing process.

Could it be possible that many alcoholics and drug addicts are victims of earthbound spirits continuing their life experiences by foisting their addictions on unsuspecting humans? Could some cases of paralysis and other illnesses actually be caused by invisible entities who are still experiencing their physical problems through human bodies because they have not yet realized they have lost their own? Is it possible that people are being institutionalized and labeled schizophrenic, manic/depressive, and so forth, when in fact they may have lost control of their bodies for various reasons to invisibles who are expressing their own ideas and behaviors through these unfortunates? Conscious evolution demands that nonmaterial reality be seriously studied and that all human experience—no matter how bizarre it may appear—must be investigated, not just labeled and conveniently ignored.

We need to know more about all the dimensions of experiences if we are to move forward in terms of the conscious evolution of humankind. Our present self-image as mere bodies is quite limiting, and is causing increasing dissension among us. With more thorough investigation of human experience, we may be able to arrive at a more correct self-image. Our bodies' material structure and boundaries seem to get in the way of our recognition of our unity with all life. However, an underlying unitive experience may emerge from a serious consideration that bodies are moving masses of atoms spinning at certain frequencies in a fluidic universal energy field. Ancient and modern mystics have repeatedly affirmed that we are not bodies—we simply possess bodies. There is great freedom and liberation in considering this possible alternative view of human existence.

The Value of Aloneness

In order to know more about our human experiences on an individual basis we may have to learn to spend more time alone considering our own inconsistencies and problems, rather than everyone else's. A Louis Harris survey reported that in the 1980s 30 percent of our population over the age of 65—eight million Americans—live alone. Of these, more than three-quarters are women, and 81 percent are widowed. Over half have lived alone for a decade or more, and nine out of ten said they preferred to live alone. Even though they experience all the hardships of daily life with fixed incomes, they value their self-reliance and independence. They no longer have their family life, but many do not feel alone. Freed of family responsibilities, they can volunteer their services, cooperate with others on constructive projects and ideas, and participate in enterprises they had no time for in the past. Social cooperation permits the full development and utilization of human power. This is one reason people seem to be at their best when they are pitching in to help one another through an emergency. People seem to receive great benefit and joy by serving and participating in their communities. But such service must emerge from conscious choice—not from a misplaced sense of obligation or guilt.

From Self-Consciousness to Universal Consciousness

Although self-consciousness will remain a human trait, we are now evolving to a more unitive consciousness. We are experiencing a fundamental shift in the way we comprehend reality, and when enough of us agree about that reality, that belief will become reality as we know it.

As self-conscious beings, our first sensing of self as distinct from everything else is accompanied by fear. As we feel danger and menace to the self, our instincts for self-preservation come into play. Our personalities are formed on wholly self-centered attitudes, and we seek those things that lead to our security, comfort, and power. Our instincts or emotions are driving forces. If we experience any resistance to our desires, we fight to overcome it. But when we begin to struggle and experience conflict, we also begin to feel separated from others.

In the Bible, we read that we are made in the image of God. If we then make God into our image as a man in isolation, we limit God. It is for us to realize the God-like qualities within ourselves if we are to understand what being "made in the image of God" means. The intention of the scripture seems to be to get us to imagine our infinite potential. I cannot limit God to merely the most powerful person I know because I see purposiveness and order in nature. It leads me to believe that purposiveness and order exist in me. As I move toward this orderly purpose, I begin to know and feel a calmness, which then provides me the opportunity to observe clearly my thoughts, actions, character, intention, habits, motivations, and all the things that make life worth living on this planet.

A friend sent the following affirmation to me, and I would like to share it with you.

Something in you knows that you are greater than anything you have yet experienced or expressed. This inner knowing, this feeling of potential greatness, is the Spirit of God in you trying to break through. It is like sunlight that may be temporarily hidden behind clouds; but the clouds cannot take away the Light. Nothing can erase or lessen the bright, glorious, wonderful spirit that is in you.

Any approach that aids you in discovering your personal truth and potential is valid. One can explore the self through mental pursuits, athletic activities, emotional therapeutic sessions, or spiritual quests. The only commitment should be—not to limit your investigations.

There are those who speak about the possibilities of revolution by expanded consciousness. Signs of an emerging positive consciousness are often ridiculed by those who promote the apathy, despair, and war machines we see multiplying all around us. And yet, right beside those who live for the benefits they might receive from lust, power, and greed, live those who are experiencing a growing awareness that is leading them toward changing personal values and gaining knowledge and liberation. We may see the power-hungry people resist, but all are being affected. This change in consciousness is taking place in all of us whether we know it or not. For instance, someone laughed at the metaphysical idea that I could attract what I wanted in my life, but at that very instant they were attracting all sorts of conflicts and disorder in their lives, and it was fairly apparent how they were doing it. Do you catch a cold when everyone else does? I don't chase one. If I want a day off, I take a day off.

The Joy of Work

Part of this revolution includes rediscovery of non-alienating work. Wouldn't it be wonderful to work at something you really enjoy doing and receive success and wealth? Your success will come at your point of interest. If you are not interested in your job, do something you like doing so you will not ruin everyone else's day with whom you come in contact because you don't want to be where you are. If people were doing what they wanted to do, it would increase world peace magnificently. But first you have to know what you want to do, and make the effort to do it successfully. Many conscious individuals have already made this transition.

More people are becoming entrepreneurs. They are creating their own work lives out of a desire to function from their point of interest where abundance and love can flow through their labor. Work is no longer a chore for them; it is a challenging source of satisfaction and joy. They are no longer working *for* a living—their work is an important part of living.

Real change can come about as we take a fresh look at who we are and what we are doing here. A major change is needed in how we perceive ourselves. With this fundamental shift in perception, other humanistic values will be introduced. The only possible source of such values is from each of us. Values and reality decided by mass agreement. We are now agreeing that the more nuclear weapons we have, the safer we will be. At this point, we have to come out of apathy and reorder assumptions or the world will perish. Our future society will probably be based on technology, but we *can* learn to use technology to serve human needs, not to destroy human beings. There is no logical or justifiable reason for hunger on this planet, or for the millions of refugees and homeless.

As different values are agreed upon, we will need

symbols and metaphors to communicate these values quickly to people. For instance, a dollar sign means money to almost anyone in the world, but what is the symbol for human kindness? Buttons with a smiling face are at least a start, but more powerful symbols are needed. People need positive identifications and reinforcements. The media, by and large, are presenting a negative identification or negative reinforcement.

We see how clearly sex, violence, and criminal activity is displayed on TV. Producers and directors could be just as explicit in demonstrating acts of kindness. We see the destructive power of deceit in detail, but how often do we get to see the positive power and benefits from honest interactions? Many of us have yet to learn how to act in loving ways, both giving and receiving. The media could more often portray kind, loving actions between individuals in depth, detailing motivations, expectations, and honesty. Through such presentations we could learn how to appreciate and praise one another. Receiving another's love may be the most loving act one can perform. Could we imagine television teaching us to learn to receive love consciously and graciously?

The media usually do not portray kind emotional responses in detail in a teaching manner. By the same token, they do not portray the positive values of "paranormal" abilities. When such paranormal subjects as healing are chosen for media presentation, whether it be fiction, magazines, TV, movies, or stage plays, the themes usually portray fraudulent activities or fatal outcomes. For instance, poltergeist and possession cases are frightening, but the sensationalism of the horror genre today goes far beyond case reports in scientific journals. For instance, the film *The Exorcist* was based on a real-life case. However, are we to believe that one's head can actually do a 360-degree turn with no damage to spine or nerves? Isn't it enough to know that a 200-pound piece of furniture can move eight feet across a floor or that a dining table can rise even inches off the floor? Facts already ascertained are astounding enough to shake the foundation of our present-day societal concept of reality; they do not need embellishment.

Next, let's look at how psychokinesis (PK), commonly called "mind over matter," is presented by the media. Movies such as *Psychic Killer* and *The Fury*, show that anger can be transmuted into PK energy which is then directed at an enemy with death as its aim. PK may arise from some type of conflict energy as one possible source, but one would have to be very skilled to be able to move a solid object weighing even a few ounces a short distance whenever he chooses to do so. Do we really want to believe that we are powerful enough to cause someone's death merely by thought? Do we think the victim has no power? Can we bear the guilt of this kind of thinking? As heads flew off bodies on the screen, presumably by PK power, audiences laughed and cheered. Encouraging this kind of expanded consciousness is a gruesome thought indeed.

How many presentations have you seen on film or television where people are healed by PK or through love and prayer? True, these types of stories are seen occasionally, but most media-featured healers are con artists out to fleece a well-to-do family through fraudulent techniques and emotional manipulation when family members are distraught and will try anything to save their loved one. Even Marcus Welby (once the epitome of the AMA) knew immediately that anyone purporting to be a healer was a fraud.

By the way, the AMA labels healing "spontaneous remission," probably employed in the cause of exclusivity rights. During the witch hunts of the 16th and 17th centuries, many so-called witches were healers who had to be done away with so that the medical profession, with its barbaric and inhumane early treatments, could be established without interference. If anyone exhibited mental disorder in the 19th century, it was assumed by "doctors" that they were possessed by a demon. Did doctors pray over patients to release the evil influence? No. They chained them, beat them, starved them, and even drilled holes in patients' heads or cut off the ends of their fingers to let demons out!

How are we to evolve out of the various forms of barbarism that exist today? Become informed. If you are not happy with your life or the life of your planet, get involved with others who are talking about solutions to problems in which you are interested. There are marvelous books today in plain language discussing every sort of human problem and possible alternatives and solutions.

Human Evolution Research—Now

The earliest question in psychic research was probably, "Do we survive death?" Today my question is, "Can we experience life with its full potential—psychic and otherwise?" Or, must we be herded like cattle into mental and spiritual corrals where we dare not explore our innate powers and abilities for personal fulfillment? Is the establishment really afraid that human beings will get out of line if we understand our essential beingness? It has been my experience that people use psychic abilities and spiritual qualities to help and heal in most instances. Lies and weapons are used to hinder and kill. As we educate ourselves about our creative, invisible potential, we will begin to demand a more accurate presentation of psychic and spiritual topics by the media.

However, it isn't only the media that are misinforming or distorting information concerning our emerging invisible abilities. Parapsychologists could well be holding us back in our conscious evolutionary process by minimizing ESP phenomena through statistical approaches and by using mystifying language to obscure information presented to the public.

There is a need now for bold *human evolution researchers* who are motivated by a desire to advance the conscious evolutionary process and who are willing and able to transmit intelligible information to the public. These researchers could take their positions on the edge of conceptual reality, access information that fits onto what we already know, and lead us into our innate expanded awareness and abilities.

Out-of-body experiences have been reported from every time period, place, culture, nationality, age group, socioeconomic class, and religion. Yet available research on this topic would suggest a much more limited experience of this phenomenon. In the field of psychic research, I detected a certain sense of exclusivity of its members and suppression of data from the "masses." It seems there is an idea that such data wouldn't be understood by most people or that it would be distorted. Are we to believe that only a few hundred people—parapsychologists—on this planet have the capacity to seriously consider our invisible abilities and potential?

I've seen people from Arizona to Appalachia to East Harlem use ESP in their daily lives while the scientists sit around and question whether a certain demonstration was clairvoyant, telepathic, precognitive, or fraud. They are falling into the trap of thinking that if you can name something, you know about it. Parapsychological nomenclature is not infallible; in fact, it often merely serves to confuse more important issues.

We see order and purpose in nature from our studies of the life cycles of galaxies to the witnessing of daily tide times and levels. Nature has a purpose for each of us. Airplanes fly according to natural laws of aerodynamics, which are invariable. It is not difficult to suppose that there are unknown natural laws in our presence that allow us to do all sorts of what-might-be-considered miracles. When something "miraculous" happens, we may call it paranormal, but it isn't! It is merely an experience beyond the limits of what is presently considered normal in this society. Reorder assumptions, remove self-imposed limitations, and liberate yourself from absurdity by claiming your own conscious awakening—now.

Natural laws and invisible forces have been understood and harnessed in inventions like radio, TV, and so forth. We can obtain a plastic card in the U.S. that offers us economic freedom wherever we go on the planet. The level of commercial trust is expanded by these devices. We have translated invisible forces into physical uses, but we value the physical comfort and generally ignore the underlying invisible principle. A shift of values seems essential if our current self-image is to evolve.

I am an invisible being. You are an invisible being. We are created equal in our invisible form. We can create anything out of this invisible reality. Buckminster Fuller emphasized before his death that our only crisis in this country is our inability to deal with invisible reality. I agree wholeheartedly.

Can you help make things go right when you are in the midst of turmoil or confusion? When there is destructive behavior all around, can you stand up for constructive purposes that will benefit the majority of those present? There are those on the planet who are content to discuss the troubles of the world and the reasons for them. There are others who feel impotent in the face of the increasingly disastrous conditions on Earth. There are some who are busy on a daily basis exploiting and capitalizing on our planetary woes. These people will even try to prevent change because it will cut into their profits. And there are also those who will stand up for truth and justice and constructive life on the planet despite ridicule, invalidation, and denial of personal rights. Where do you stand?

This is the only life we know about right now, and this planet is the only home we know in this universe. If someone were stealing my child, I would do everything I could to get her back. No matter how difficult, no matter how many of my friends advised me to discontinue my search, I would probably never give up trying to find and save my child.

This Earth is an entity that has been entrusted to us, much as a child would be. We need to be aware of it, and care for it daily. Therefore, no matter how discouraged you are by the threats of the death of the planet, do not stop trying to save it and yourself along with it. Do everything you can every day—whether it be in your mind or in your neighborhood—to save the planet. Fully evolved people raise consciousness wherever they go and bring people out of apathy into the revolution—and this will eventually bring us to our next stage of conscious evolution.

Chapter 8
End Notes

[1]W. J. Finch, *The Pendulum & Possession*. Jerome, AZ: Luminary Press, 1975.

[2]Carl A. Wickland, *Thirty Years Among the Dead*. Van Nuys, CA: Newcastle Publishing Co., 1974.

Chapter IX

CONSCIOUS EVOLUTION: WHY BOTHER?

Evolution as conscious beings is a process of continuous change to a better state of being—it moves us toward a vision of good. It cannot be otherwise unless we get stuck somewhere along the way temporarily. Even then we will eventually free ourselves and move on to another experience. Why bother to evolve "consciously"? Because we have begun to recognize the fallacy of self-conscious thinking. Because we wish to move out of the mire of fear, pain, and shame. Because we want to move toward the ideals of freedom, justice, and goodwill for all and know we can't get there by merciless violence and greed. And because we have come to see the value in unselfishness, kindliness, and cooperation.

This desire to move forward together often develops after we get a brief glimpse of another reality or have a spontaneous experience of a spiritual nature. We get a feeling that there is more to life than meets the eye and we want to know what it is. We are impatient to feel our connection and value to the entire system. The possibility of eventually having a sense of belonging pulls us onward. This is when we begin to realize that our extended sensory capacities are a better way of gaining information. We suspect there is a fundamental unity of all things, and that time and evil are illusions. That's when we begin to grasp the adventure that life can be.

We do not evolve merely to fulfill a need for adventure and excitement. We evolve because we are human beings, a part of all nature, and that's what nature does. We are involved in the evolutionary process because we are the only beings we know who can be conscious of evolution.

Physicist Raynor Johnson studied psychic research and mysticism for many years and in his book *The Imprisoned Splendour* made this suggestion:

> ...the creative activity of God includes embryonic spiritual beings, entities having simple consciousness, which is, however, infinite and eternal. The maturing of these so that they come to *know* their divinity (which they already possess, but do not realize they possess) is perhaps the basis of the whole cycle of Becoming....
>
> An acorn retains all the potentialities of the oak from which it came, but they are latent and unmanifest until it is sown in the earth and subject to the forces and buffetings of the kingdom below it. From this it emerges, climbing into the light, to become ultimately another mature oak. It is perhaps a faint analogy of the process of growth of embryonic spirit sown in the lower strata of mind and matter and subject to all the buffetings of experience.[1]

The value and importance of spiritual and intuitive experiences are underestimated in our verbal- and sensory-dominated society. It is important for us to know more about our human experiences in order to move forward in our own evolutionary process.

The Challenge of Reordering Assumptions

Since the beginning of recorded history, humans have suspected the existence of some part of ourselves that is generally unrecognized and unexpressed. We see intimations of it in literature from every age. More importantly, everyone reading this book has probably had an experience that clearly demonstrates the presence of an invisible part of humankind. For instance, I cannot remember your name in the morning; I can in the afternoon. I was sure I knew your name, but I couldn't access the information that morning. Where was the memory, and why was it temporarily dislocated?

Despite all the written information on the unconscious and common experiences that suggested its existence, the concept of the unconscious did not make the slightest impact on society until Freud. His theories changed our human self-image. He created this tremendous, psychological impact because he did two important things. First, he analyzed the unconscious in terms that fit the spirit of his times, which made quite a sensation. Second, he turned the concept into a culturally useful tool for self-transformation—psychoanalysis. We did not accept the unconscious part of ourselves as having any influence in our lives until Freud did these two things.

We now accept the unconscious as a part of our daily experience. You would probably be amazed to meet anyone today who didn't know or at least believe there was an unconscious part of the human mind. This acceptance of more of ourselves has led to considerable changes in education, medicine, art, child-rearing practices, law, and so forth. When you change concepts, you change behavior.

Lawrence LeShan, who wrote *Alternate Realities* and other books and articles on these topics, has studied psychoanalytic theory, ESP, and psychic beingness. He addresses issues of reordering assumptions and changing concepts. He feels our challenge today is whether or not we can accept ourselves as part of the energy of the universe and function harmoniously with it and each other. He writes that there seems to be:

> ...a force, an energy, that binds the cosmos together and moves always in the direction of its harmonious action and the fruition of the separate connected parts. In [people] this force emerges and expresses itself as love, and this is the "spark of the divine" in each of us.
>
> When this force is acknowledged and reinforced by the culture, it is possible for human beings to relate harmoniously to themselves, to others, to the rest of the cosmos, and to move toward the most unique and awesome self-fulfillment.
>
> When this force is ignored or discouraged, the energy becomes blocked and distorted, and in all human history has been expressed in self-hatred, a hunger for power, materialistic greed, and ultimately, as the dehumanization of our time makes clear, in the real possibility of man's so disrupting the expression of his energy as to end his part in the cosmic design.[2]

In the arena of psychic research, facts have been discovered that contradict the assumptions on which we base our physical interpretation of humans as individual automatons. ESP facts do not confirm separateness; these exceptional facts could lead us into greater self-knowledge.

ESP itself may be incorrectly identified. These abilities may be much more a primary perception than an extrasensory one. ESP data lead us to perceive the world and ourselves in a different way. If we are only what we have been taught to believe we are, ESP data would not exist. LeShan described it this way:

> If [we] were only flesh and bone, if [we] worked on the same type of principle as a machine, and if [we] were as separate from [each other] as we have thought, it would be impossible for [us] to do the things we know [we] sometimes [do].[3] [Author provided nonsexist language.]

The real importance of ESP is that it allows us a peek at what we can be and, in fact, are.

Psychic research has given us clues and clear indications for a different human concept, based on in-depth studies of extraordinary human experiences. The concept is still a little difficult for most of us to grasp because it flies in the face of our preconceptions, as well as what we think of as our experience. However, this is a significant discrepancy. It is comparable to the revolutionary ideas put forth by Copernicus and Columbus. They tried to lead people out of false assumptions that the Sun rotated around the Earth, and that the Earth was flat. It was not easy to influence people to change their opinions when they considered their ideas to be based on common sense. Everyone saw the Sun rise and set, and believed that if the Earth were round, those on the bottom would fall off. They thought we were sustained on Earth because it was flat; they had never heard of a law of gravity. These are examples of preconceptions that have now been dismissed with the acceptance of more recent scientific knowledge disclosing facts that were previously invisible, such as the force of gravity.

ESP phenomena just don't fit in with commonsense beliefs about the way things work. They are dissonant facts, somewhat uncomfortable, like dissenting opinions. Scientists fear that if these facts are admitted, they will disrupt the scheme of the known and familiar. In other words, their precious theories may be proved inadequate. We have a tremendous investment in our materialistic and mechanistic concept of reality. If we accept ESP, it threatens our present view of ourselves. We fear that our personality structure may not survive the change.

People have told me that evidence of ESP "threatens their reality." In truth, your present reality is under no real threat when you take in new information. For instance, I can still stand on flat ground even though I no longer believe the Earth is flat. I can now see the Earth as both flat and round. I have expanded my ideas of reality, not destroyed them. Some people feel defenseless in the face of telepathy as a reality. One of LeShan's clients said, "All my life experiences make no sense if such an important thing exists and I never knew it."

Since the 19th century, people who have taken an active interest in parapsychology have had their names discredited, have been denied positions for which they were qualified, and have had their ability to think rationally questioned, but

> There are far too many individuals with courage and scientific conviction to permit data and concepts of this magnitude to be suppressed by social stigma and discrimination.[4]

Sensitives, some of whom have faced death for their beliefs, have provided us with a wealth of information about their realities. They describe their terrain as "a fundamental shift of one's awareness" or "the field of stimulation is itself changed." They agree, along with those who have studied mysticism, that there are four basic characteristics to this different conception of reality. They are:

1. Expanded sensory awareness is a better way of gaining information.
2. There is a fundamental unity to all things.
3. Time is an illusion.
4. All evil is an appearance.

These sensitives had great courage and withstood enormous societal prejudice and ridicule. But they were on a personal adventure and had a zest for life. Famed medium Eileen Garrett entitled one of her best books *My Life as a Search for the Meaning of Mediumship*. She was totally dedicated to her search for knowledge, to her evolution as a creative invisible being. It is not unusual for a person who follows the mystical path or spiritual disciplines to find joy, serenity, and a nondestructive life of peace and fulfillment of purpose.

Being Truly Alive

For some, fear of knowing the self may cause extreme anxiety. If we become aware of personal insights, we may be exposed to information we are ill-prepared to assimilate. It may take a considerable amount of time and effort changing comfortable habits of thought and action that do not produce desired effects. Some feel it's better not to know about their unconscious drives and feelings. They may not choose to know about potentialities not fulfilled or self-actualization not attained. What good is it to have all this knowledge about oneself, anyway?

As children we may have felt at home here on the planet and acted spontaneously without fear, but for most of us this spontaneity was repressed early in life. Every time parents tell a child not to think, feel, say or do something, a part of the child gets submerged. Sometimes we long for that part of us that got pushed aside and buried, that went unrecognized and unexpressed. But what difference does it make? LeShan writes:

> The price for denying a basic part of one's being is well known to Western psychological science today—its cost is in diminished joy and zest, in a tendency toward pathological symptoms, hate and destruction, self-hate, and self-contempt.[5]

Are we ready to destroy humanity because of our ignorance of our true selves? British psychic investigator and novelist Colin Wilson seems to believe that:

> One of the chief obstacles to human evolution is man's boredom and ignorance, his tendency to drift and allow tomorrow to take care of itself.... Once man has a purpose and a belief, he is almost invincible.[6]

We are at a point of evolution where we are on the brink of achieving additional power. Tremendous energies are being generated on earth at this time by our evolutionary struggle. At the same time as we seek to discover the inner worlds within ourselves, the physical world is forever demanding our attention. Yet, if we resist these mental distractions, we might experience a sense of peace or mental balance unknown to us before; we might not feel so suppressed or oppressed by externals; and we might experience a fresh surge of energy and optimism. We might get in touch with the inner powers we possess and possibly begin to utilize the most remarkable faculty human beings have in their power—creativity.

Do you remember the times in your life when you felt you were truly alive?

I feel the power of my being when I feel strong in body and mind, and when my heart is filled with joy. I can become aware of this power any time I turn to it in honesty, humility, and gratitude. There is a basic human need for creative self-expression, whether it be an Appalachian woman quilting or Michelangelo painting the Sistine Chapel. When we allow our creativity to express itself in any form, it feels good. Our feelings of inadequacy are suspended for a time and are replaced by relief and joy.

Maybe some of you have felt yourself in unity with another person's mind? This is not an uncommon experience. Remember the sense of exhilaration and power you both felt? You really knew for an instant that you *were* each other in some real way. Try to get an image of the whole human race (five billion Earthlings) in this kind of mental unity. Think of the power that could be generated if we combined our wills and focused our attention to common purposes.

God—"New and Improved"

There's a lot of talk today about new thought, new age, and so forth. Our consumer society is hooked on anything new. As many years as we have been buying products that are "NEW AND IMPROVED," the advertising technique still seems to work. In the book of Ecclesiastes in the Old Testament it is written that, "There is nothing new under the sun"—and the modern derivative is, "Everything that goes around, comes around." Perhaps rather than always wanting something "new and improved," our emphasis might be better placed on how we can actually utilize what comes and goes in the moment.

One thing that we are getting in the so-called "New Age" is a much more present and powerful image of God. God is no longer a male entity sitting far away on a cloud in the sky, but rather a presence as close and as meaningful as the air we breathe. More and more conscious people are beginning to feel that they *are* a part of all that is. The idea of separation from one's power and good is breaking down rapidly. Once we appreciate that we have access to all there is or ever has been or will ever be, it will be up to each of us to accept whatever we can have comfortably.

An example of this principle in operation might be the individuals who attain success and fame and then can't cope with having more and more of everything at their disposal. We see more than a few of the rich and famous sabotage themselves at this level, even to the point of self-destruction. As you move along this path of conscious evolution, you will need to know how to accept your good and use your power for *the highest good for the most people.*

God might be envisioned as an invisible, all-encompassing, passive benevolence that is all around us and within us, essential to all life and substance—a power, an energy that can be recognized, internalized, personalized, and expressed. In this conception, God is an integral part of us, existing as our potential self. Our goal might be to become conscious of that potential, to gain knowledge of its purpose, and then to get into action energized by that source.

In order to free ourselves for this kind of powerful living, we may have to seek out and change unconscious habits that are self-destructive. Animals live on reflex and habit; their behavior is governed by unconscious instinct. Some humans operate in this way to varying extents, but we also have self-consciousness—we can choose. We have the ability to change our behavior and do something different and original. We can limit ourselves to habitual existence, or we can accept our godliness and operate through grace from an invisible, creative level. It's our choice. Unfortunately, we seem to have lost our personal identity in this materialistic consumer society. We will have to pay more attention to the vast potential of human experience if we are to move forward in our spiritual evolution.

The Grand Adventure

Life can be a grand adventure as you enter into the realms of your mind and beingness. Throw off the shackles of a personal image someone else created for you. Come to know your essential being and *be* that.

I rode the subways of New York for over twenty years. I was told they were unsafe and disgusting, but I thought it was a great way to get around, and I usually studied on my long rides from Brooklyn to other boroughs of the city. I was not immune to the cosmopolitan atmosphere and enjoyed the many different languages, colors, styles, and nationalities of my fellow passengers. I was part of this great melting pot; time and space often did not exist as I experienced this unity of purpose. We had a power, a vehicle, greater than ourselves—the subway—taking each of us to our desired destination. Those people who dreaded being on the subway, hating everything and everybody who wasn't like them, counting each stop and yawning with boredom, had to live through each unpleasant moment and every endless mile. We each had the same external experience, but internally our experiences were totally different. It is the internal experience that governs how you perceive the external.

Colin Wilson, in his wonderful novel, *The Mind*

Parasites, speaks of the intensity and control one might experience as a result of focusing on the invisible creative aspects of one's being:

> It became clear that there is a fundamental *mistake* about ordinary human existence—as absurd as trying to fill a bath with the plug out, or driving a car with the hand brake on.... The mind begins to brim with a sense of vitality and control. Instead of being at the mercy of moods and feelings, we control them as easily as we control the movements of our hands. The result can hardly be described to anyone who has not experienced it. Human beings get so used to things "happening" to them. They catch cold; they feel depressed; they pick something up and drop it; they experience boredom.... But once I had turned my attention into my own mind, these things ceased to happen, because I now controlled them.[7]

As we improve our conscious contact with everything that is, we no longer only perceive things as happening *to* us, but as happening *through* us. In this case, we have something to say about the matter. I've never quite understood why people are so concerned about controlling someone else's life and body, while having so little interest in controlling their own.

Conscious evolution involves positive and constructive thinking, talking, and acting. Growth involves an outward or upward movement—stagnation is inactive and motionless. That which we call evil can be considered in a sense an outer reflection of our inner cowardice and passivity. It thrives on an atmosphere of defeat and panic because it feeds on human fear. One way to combat evil would seem to be to change our personal and planetary emotional atmosphere to one of strength and purpose.

Learning to Walk

Our future evolution depends on our willingness to identify ourselves as creative invisible beings. The existence of extrasensory abilities—including telepathy (mind-to-mind communication), precognition (knowledge of the future), clairvoyance (information about distant objects and events), and psychokinesis (mind over matter)—have now been scientifically established. The bulk of data collected on these abilities for the past hundred years using scientific techniques would have been sufficient to cause scientists in any other field to accept their phenomena as genuine.

The Parapsychological Association was admitted into membership in the American Association for the Advancement of Science in 1969. Even though this scientific affiliation has been established for twenty years, the phenomena are still questioned within scientific circles, as well as in the general public.

People still seem reluctant to take personal responsibility for their expanded human abilities. We seem to be afraid that these abilities are dangerous or that they will only be used to manipulate or destroy. This fear, in turn, causes us to repress or suppress such abilities, whether one is a scientist in a laboratory who minimizes abilities by only reporting them as statistics, or an individual who refers to psychic experiences as uncanny, coincidental, or weird.

Just remember, we didn't learn to walk overnight. Learning to experience and accept our extrasensory perceptions and abilities is also going to take time, effort, and lots of falling down and getting up. But consider how different your world would be if you had never taken the opportunity to learn to walk. Imagine how limited your life experience would be.

I believe that, until we learn to walk as fully expanded creative beings, our life experience will continue to be equally limited at this important juncture in our evolutionary progress.

Eight Principles of Conscious Evolution

1. **BECOME A CONSCIOUS OBSERVER OF YOUR THOUGHTS, FEELINGS AND BEHAVIOR. ASK PERTINENT QUESTIONS, SUCH AS "WHO IS DOING THE OBSERVING?" "WHO AM I?" "WHAT AM I TO DO?" EXPECT INFORMATION TO ARRIVE IN SOME FORM TO ENLIGHTEN YOU CONCERNING YOUR QUESTIONS.**

As you observe your thoughts, feelings, and behavior, you will know more about who you are, what you are interested in, and how you would like to express yourself. It will also be good to keep a check on your motivations and expectations. Why do you behave in a certain way? What do you hope to get out of thinking along certain lines? You may receive answers to these questions from intuition, or you may talk to another person who will give you pertinent information about yourself that you may not have been able to see clearly before. Information can come from books, newspapers, TV, a phone call, an accidental meeting with a stranger. Don't rule out any means of communication as a possible source for the information you are seeking. Pay attention internally and externally. Knowledge is available, we have access to it. What we want to do now is to become conscious of its presence in our lives and welcome it!

2. **BE AS HONEST WITH YOURSELF AS YOU POSSIBLY CAN. DECIDE WHETHER YOUR OBSERVATIONS ARE REAL-**

ITY BASED (POSSIBLE AND WORKABLE) OR FANTASY (DREAMING AS OPPOSED TO PLANNING).

Don't delude yourself into thinking you are more or less important than you really are. You are a valuable part of this universe—it would not be the same without your presence. If an idea or behavior isn't working for you, realize that and don't blame it on someone else or you may waste hours of mental energy resenting some person or situation. You have better things to do with your limited time on this planet. Self-honesty is of utmost importance in keeping your balance as you move through the changes of your conscious evolutionary process. You might want to keep a journal to document your experiences. This valuable tool can also be used to search out the larger patterns of your behavior.

3. **EXAMINE ANY IDEA ABOUT YOURSELF THAT MAKES YOU FEEL UNCOMFORTABLE—ANY SELF-CONCEPT THAT ISN'T WORKING FOR YOU. CONSIDER WHETHER THIS IS REALLY THE TRUTH ABOUT YOU RIGHT NOW, OR WHETHER IT'S SOMETHING THAT SOMEONE ELSE SUGGESTED TO YOU OR PROJECTED ONTO YOU.**

I know writers who tell me that if they only had a computer they could write. Without the computer they are unhappy because they can't write. And because they are not expressing themselves, they're not receiving remuneration for their talents. There is a false assumption operating here: "I can't write without a computer." Because of this false assumption their whole lives are not working. They had heard that most authors put their books on computers. But the truth is they don't need a computer—all they need to write is paper and a pen or pencil. As the words begin to flow, the necessary equipment will be provided for the complete expression of that person's abilities. (Read *Child of the Dark: The Diary of Carolina Maria de Jesus*, if you don't believe this.) Operating at this level requires faith and experimentation. Don't put any obstacles between you and the expression of your self or the desires of your heart.

4. LEARN TO TRUST YOUR EXPANDED HUMAN ABILITIES, SUCH AS INTUITION OR INNER GUIDANCE.

Can you trust yourself? Are you afraid that you will deceive yourself if you depend on more subtle forms of information and knowing? Fear is a major obstacle to conscious evolution, but through positive outcomes achieved by trusting our inner guidance and direct knowing ability, we can learn how to accept our invisible information channels with the same confidence we accept messages from sensory channels. Start with low-risk situations for learning to gain confidence with your inner guidance.

For instance, if you get on a train or bus going in the wrong direction for where you thought you were going, be alert for an unexpected favorable event. Maybe you will see someone you have been wanting to see; maybe you will get information you need, but didn't consciously know how to get; or maybe you will learn you have avoided an unfavorable event through your error. If we can learn to trust at this level, it may be easier to trust our extrasensory perceptions of people and other external information. Knowledge can come from anywhere at any time, and we want to be ready to receive it and not cast it aside because of false preconceptions about the way things "should be."

5. EXPERIMENT WITH AND PRACTICE YOUR EXPANDED ABILITIES, SUCH AS TELEPATHY, CLAIRVOYANCE PSYCHOKINESIS, PRECOGNITIVE DREAMING, DIRECT UNCONSCIOUS KNOWING, AND MANIFESTATION THROUGH VISUALIZATIONS.

Here's an example of experimenting with manifestation through visualization: Try to think a different, positive thought about something you desire. Instead of thinking of all the reasons you can't have it or be it or do it, think of the joy the fulfillment of your desire would bring you, and how you deserve it, and how it will improve the quality of your life. See yourself in your mind's eye in the ideal situation. If a thought comes by that "this is ridiculous," hold it in abeyance for a while as you clearly visualize this new state of being, having, or doing. If a critical voice speaks up and tells you that you do not deserve it, quiet that voice down for the moment. Be true to your ideal. Expect your desire to be actualized.

6. ACKNOWLEDGE AND VALIDATE YOUR ESP EXPERIENCES. ONE WAY TO VALIDATE YOUR ESP IS TO FACTUALLY VERIFY INFORMATION RECEIVED IN THE EXPERIENCE LATER ON. ANOTHER RULE OF THUMB MIGHT BE, IF IT IMPROVES YOUR LIFE CONDITION, IT IS VALID.

It is most important as you actually demonstrate your ESP abilities that you *not* make statements, such as the following, to yourself or others.

"It's weird, but this happened to me."
"What a coincidence!"
"I can't believe I did that."

"How uncanny that I should have dreamed about that the other night and today it happened."

"You're going to think I'm crazy when I tell you this, but..."

Consider the possibility that focused thinking and speaking puts energy into the atmosphere to create the intended object, event, or state of mind. After a few experiments, identify what it was you wanted to manifest. Note what steps you took to make your demonstration successful, and the date on which the actual manifestation occurred. In time, you will either decide that this is a bunch of nonsense, or that it actually works. Without skeptical examination, you can decide neither. If it works for you, acknowledge your ability—that way it will be able to expand and become more instantaneous and exact.

7. **BECOME CONSCIOUS OF THE SOURCE OF GREATER KNOWLEDGE AND POWER WITHIN YOU. ALLOW THAT SOURCE OF KNOWLEDGE AND POWER TO OPERATE THROUGH YOU AND GUIDE YOU TO YOUR HIGHEST GOOD. ACCEPT YOUR REWARDS JOYOUSLY.**

Without the idea of some power greater than yourself, your efforts at conscious evolution may be wasted in ego gratification. Opinion leaders from every field of endeavor affirm the presence of a supreme being of some nature. Allow yourself time to be quiet, to let go of daily tension, to give your inner guidance an opportunity to make itself known to you. Look for beauty, purpose, and order all around you. Your reward will be an increasing appreciation and reverence for life.

8. SAY THANK YOU!

CHAPTER 9
END NOTES

[1]Raynor C. Johnson, *The Imprisoned Splendour*. New York: Harper & Row, 1953, pp. 402–403.

[2]Lawrence LeShan, *The Medium, The Mystic, and the Physicist*. New York: Viking Press, 1974, pp. 166–167.

[3]*Ibid.*, p. 11.

[4]*Ibid.*, p. 215.

[5]*Ibid.*, p. 100.

[6]Colin Wilson, *The Mind Parasites*. Berkeley, CA: Oneiric Press, 1979, p. 68.

[7]*Ibid.*, pp. 87–88.

BIBLIOGRAPHY

Bickerton, D. 1985. *Roots of Language*. Ann Arbor, MI: Karoma.

Bowles, N. F. Hynds. 1978. *Psi Search*. New York: Harper & Row.

Bruner, J. S. 1968. *Processes of Cognitive Growth: Infancy*. Worcester, MA: Clark University Press.

Burt, C. 1967. "Psychology and Parapsychology." In *Science and ESP* edited by J. R. Smythies. New York: Humanities Press.

Chomsky, N. 1968. *Language and Mind*. New York: Harcourt Brace Jovanovich.

de Jesus, C. M. 1962. *Child of the Dark: The Diary of Carolina Maria de Jesus*. New York: Signet.

Fiore, E. 1987. *The Unquiet Dead: A Psychologist Treats Spirit Possession*. New York: Ballantine.

Fuller, B. 1963. *Ideas and Integrities: A Spontaneous Autobiographical Disclosure*. New York: Collier Books.

Garrett, E. J. 1975. *My Life as a Search for the Meaning of Mediumship*. New York: Arno.

LeShan, L. 1977. *Alternate Realities*. New York: Ballantine.

Marsden, R. 1983. *Psychic Experience for You*. Great Britain: Aquarian Press.

Mishlove, J. 1983. *Psi Development Systems*. New York: Ballantine.

Piaget, J. B. Inhelder. 1969. *The Psychology of the Child*. New York: Basic Books.

Sherrington, C. S. 1940. *Man on his Nature*. London: Cambridge University Press.

Skinner, B. F. 1971. *Beyond Freedom and Dignity*. New York: Knopf.

Swann, I. 1975. *To Kiss Earth Good-Bye*. New York: Hawthorn Books.

Watson, J. B. 1919. *Psychology from the Standpoint of a Behaviorist*. Philadelphia: Lippincott.

INDEX

ABOUT THE AUTHOR

Dr. Janet Mitchell, who holds a Ph.D. in Experimental Cognition from the City University of New York, began her studies in parapsychology in 1967.

The primary objective of her work has been to advance human understanding of the essential self and its scope of abilities.

Dr. Mitchell lives in Cottonwood, Arizona.

By the same author

OUT-OF-BODY EXPERIENCES

A Handbook

What is the best, safest method to induce an OBE?

Is there a limit to how far away one should go from the body?

Is it possible to go out and not be able to get back in the body?

Do I need a teacher to learn how to have this experience?

Have astral bodies actually been photographed?

What are the main fears that hold one back from an OBE?

Based on laboratory investigations by a veteran parapsychologist, this unique book suggests that a person's conscious awareness can detach itself from the person's body and travel for an extended period of time.

It is science fact or science fiction?
Decide for yourself – with this complete guide to OBEs including:
● First person accounts ● Comprehensive history of occurrences through the ages across all cultures ● The 90 most commonly asked questions about OBEs

'An excellent introduction to this fascinating domain of human experience.'
Kenneth Ring, author of *Life After Death*